The media's watching Vault!
Here's a sampling of our coverage.

"For those hoping to climb the ladder of success, [Vault's] insights are priceless."
– *Money magazine*

"The best place on the web to prepare for a job search."
– *Fortune*

"[Vault guides] make for excellent starting points for job hunters and should be purchased by academic libraries for their career sections [and] university career centers."
– *Library Journal*

"The granddaddy of worker sites."
– *US News and World Report*

"A killer app."
– *New York Times*

One of Forbes' 33 "Favorite Sites"
– *Forbes*

"To get the unvarnished scoop, check out Vault."
– *Smart Money Magazine*

"Vault has a wealth of information about major employers and job-searching strategies as well as comments from workers about their experiences at specific companies."
– *The Washington Post*

"A key reference for those who want to know what it takes to get hired by a law firm and what to expect once they get there."
– *New York Law Journal*

"Vault [provides] the skinny on working conditions at all kinds of companies from current and former employees."
– *USA Today*

formation™

VAULT CAREER GUIDE TO THE REAL ESTATE INDUSTRY

VAULT CAREER GUIDE TO THE REAL ESTATE INDUSTRY

RAUL SAAVEDRA JR.
AND THE STAFF OF VAULT

Library of Congress Cataloging-in-Publication Data

Saavedra, Raul.
 Vault career guide to the real estate industry / Raul Saavedra, Jr. and the Staff of Vault.
   p. cm.
  ISBN 1-58131-174-5
1. Real estate business--Vocational guidance--United States. 2. Real estate agents--United States. I. Title: Career guide to the real estate industry. II. Vault (Firm) III. Title.
 HD255.S225 2003
 333.33'023'73--dc21

                                                          2003013395

Printed in the United States of America

ACKNOWLEDGEMENTS

From Raul Saavedra: There are few "thank yous" I must distribute. First, I need to thank my wife, Jennifer, who let me disappear on the weekends to get this done. Next, I need to thank the interview subjects who made themselves available to my endless questions. Also, I want to thank my former classmates and the real estate faculty at Kellogg, who took the time to proofread and offer invaluable suggestions for the book. Finally, I can't forget the staff at Vault who were flexible and taught me a great deal about writing – especially the incomparable Marcy Lerner.

From Vault: Thanks to Matt Doull, Ahmad Al-Khaled, Lee Black, Eric Ober, Hollinger Ventures, Tekbanc, New York City Investment Fund, Globix, Hoover's, Glenn Fischer, Mark Hernandez, Ravi Mhatre, Carter Weiss, Ken Cron, Ed Somekh, Isidore Mayrock, Zahi Khouri, Sana Sabbagh, and other Vault investors, as well as our family and friends.

Table of Contents

Visit Vault at www.vault.com for insider company profiles, expert advice,
career message boards, expert resume reviews, the Vault Job Board and more.

VAULT CAREER LIBRARY   **ix**

Visit Vault at **www.vault.com** for insider company profiles, expert advice,
career message boards, expert resume reviews, the Vault Job Board and more.

VAULT CAREER LIBRARY   xi

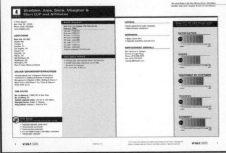

Introduction

Real estate is big money and big business. The real estate industry is home to some of the wealthiest businesspeople on the planet: Donald Trump, Leona Helmsley and Sam Zell. Yet the industry also touches each one of us, whether you're looking for a new apartment with a backyard or checking out the new "big box" store that's opening up in your city.

In the last 10 years, the domestic real estate industry has provided a critical momentum to the United States economy, which means there are some major career opportunities available. Read this guide and you'll learn more about the hottest careers in the business, from real estate brokerage to property management to high-rolling real estate finance.

THE SCOOP

Industry Overview

CHAPTER 2

What is Real Estate?

Real estate is tangible. It's a piece of land and any building or structures on it, as well as the air above and the ground below. Everyone comes into direct contact with real estate. The places we live, work, go to school, vacation, shop and exercise, are all assets to be bought, sold and rented. And it's always been an important element of the economy. As of 2001, the industry represented a whopping 11.6 percent of the gross domestic product of the United States.

History of Real Estate in the United States

Real estate has always been big business in the United States. Shortly after the signing of the Constitution, the federal government began transferring one billion acres of land to private owners through land sales and land grants. In the 1830s, for example, the government sold 20 million acres at roughly $1.25 per acre. This sounds like a bargain to us today, but at the time the vast majority of citizens couldn't afford that price. Consequently, a grassroots group called the Free Soil Movement formed and lobbied the government for an alternate method of distributing land.

The Homestead Act of 1862 was Congress' answer to the appeal. Settlers who did not already own what was considered a "judicious" amount of land were given title to 160 acres for each adult in the family. There was no cash exchange. Instead, the understanding was that the settlers would live on and improve the land for a period of at least five years. This program was very successful and similar federal land distribution programs followed until the later part of the nineteenth century. In total, the U.S. government distributed more than 300 million acres of public property to private landowners through the Homestead Act, creating the basis for the real estate market.

For the first time in the history of the young country, there was a system in place by which one landowner could transfer property rights to another through sale, lease or trade. This led to a tremendous amount of speculation. Some investors accumulated a tremendous amount of wealth, while others lost everything.

At the end of the 19th century, America was transitioning from an agricultural society to a manufacturing economy. Citizens flocked to urban areas to work at the burgeoning factories. For example, as the Midwest's industrial center, Chicago reached a population of one million people more rapidly than any other city in history. Settled in the 1830s, the city grew from less than 1,000 inhabitants to become the fifth largest city in the world by 1900.

The values of urban properties skyrocketed. By 1920, 50 percent of America's population lived in cities. This urban density created opportunities for real estate development as housing, office buildings, industrial facilities, hotels and retail centers were constructed to meet the demands of city dwellers.

Skyrocketing property values and associated costs began pushing people and businesses outside the city, just as advances in transportation made living outside the city easier. Suburbs, communities just outside urban centers, began to spread. Developers made these planned communities attractive by building along the transportation routes so people could easily commute to their jobs in the cities.

Technological advances influenced the building boom of the 1920s. Communities were wired for electricity, new machines such as elevators helped meet additional demand for space and allowed the construction of ever-taller buildings. Planned communities began taking shape in the suburbs, while skyscrapers changed the way the cities looked. One hundred buildings higher than 25 stories were constructed in this decade, most of them in New York City, with Chicago a distant second.

The Great Depression crippled most industries – including real estate. Values dipped below debt levels, causing a collapse. The federal government put the domestic financial markets through a major overhaul and was shrewd enough to include real estate financing as part of the New Deal programs. The Federal Housing Administration (FHA) was created in 1930 to provide mortgage insurance, lowering the risk on real estate loans and making lending more palatable for savings and loans and banks. The government also created the Federal Home Loan Bank System (FHLB) to supervise and regulate local banks. In 1938, the Federal National Mortgage Association (FNMA or Fannie Mae) was created to provide a secondary mortgage market as well as to lure investment capital in the mortgage market, and continues to play a very important role in supplying capital to the mortgage market today. These New Deal programs ultimately made the real estate finance market more sophisticated and secure.

America and the real estate industry slowly climbed out of the Depression only to fall headlong into the Second World War. Development was put on hold during the war, but once the GIs returned from overseas, another era of prosperity began. A tremendous amount of demand for housing emerged virtually overnight. By 1946, new housing construction quadrupled to over 500,000 homes. In the postwar period, a white picket fence and peaceful green lawn proved very appealing. Two-thirds of the 15 million homes built in the 1950s were in the suburbs.

The decade was also a period of expansion for the highways, which provided access to more areas by car and truck. This enabled all types of real estate (e.g. hotels, industrial and retail centers) to be located further outside the city. Hotel chains like Holiday Inn started popping up along roadways across the country. The suburban shopping mall also became popular in this era.

As the suburbs grew, the cities slumped. By 1960, many urban centers hadn't seen new office building development in 30 years. The decay of America's urban areas didn't go unnoticed. Community activism and political pressure led to the creation of a cabinet position in 1965 focused on improving urban housing – what today is known as the Department of Housing and Urban Development (HUD). The central business districts of America's urban centers saw a number of new buildings (both commercial and retail) constructed during the last three decades of the twentieth century, spurred by growth in the service industry, increased access to financing and municipal incentives.

Today, the real estate industry is considered one of the most dynamic and healthy sectors in the American economy – people may divest their stocks, but they always need a place to live, work and shop. (To read more about the history of real estate, read *Real Estate Development* by Miles, Berns and Weiss.)

Industry Trends

As of 2003, the real estate business employs close to five million people. Opportunities abound for candidates to earn staggering income levels. Those who work in this sector often enjoy greater flexibility in job responsibilities than in other industries.

There can be drawbacks, though, in the form of low paying entry-level positions, competitive co-workers and long hours when starting out. Furthermore, once you're established relocation can be detrimental to your career, as this industry is often geography-specific.

Visit Vault at **www.vault.com** for insider company profiles, expert advice, career message boards, expert resume reviews, the Vault Job Board and more.

VAULT CAREER LIBRARY   7

The real estate sector is largely dependent on the economy; small shifts can impact trends significantly. For example, the technology industry boom certainly helped the real estate industry in the 1990s. There was more demand for space-both commercial and residential-and asset values skyrocketed. The subsequent technology bust had a dramatic effect on some parts of the sector. Commercial firms that focused on office and retail development projects now find the market glutted with available space.

The residential real estate market is also affectecd by economic swings. Unemployment and interest rates impact both consumer confidence and buying power. Although today's economy has been mired in recession for years, the residential real estate market is considered one of the few bright spots. In 2002, home sales shot up 8 percent and housing starts grew by 7 percent. The numbers for 2003 look similarly healthy.

There are many reasons for the current residential housing boom. The aging United States population and the influx of immigrants has increased the demand for households. The rockiness of the stock market makes investing in real estate look very appealing. The Federal Reserve is playing a big part as well. Lower mortgage rates and minimal inflations means that in 2003, a 30 year home mortgage can be had at a 5 percent rate. The drop in mortgage rates means that homeowners can refinance, freeing up more cash for them – and in the process making real estate look like an even more attractive investment.

The wealth isn't spread equally. Residential real estate values continue to soar on the coasts. During the real estate boom that began after the end of the 1991 recession, homes and apartments in the Boston-to-Washington corridor and California have doubled, tripled or quadrupled in value. Even in fast-growing areas in other parts of the country, such as Las Vegas, gains have been more modest because there is more land on which to build houses and apartments.

The remarkable gains in the residential real estate market have provoked fears among some economists and homeowners that the real estate market is a bubble about to burst. The prices of homes, especially on the West and East Coast, have outpaced the ability of many prospective first-time buyers to purchase a place to live. A jump in mortgage rates would stop the current trend of refinancing in its tracks and make it more difficult for many homeowners to make mortgage payments. A revival in the economy could cause investors to stop investing in real estate and start investing in stocks. (Such a revival would, on the other hand, help the commercial and industrial real estate markets.) In the meantime, however, the residential real estate market continues to be an engine of the economy – and of the real estate job market.

Building Your Real Estate Foundation

CHAPTER 3

Real Estate: What's it Worth?

Although there are various ways to value different kinds of real estate, there are a few things that make any propery asset valuable. First there's the unofficial industy motto: "The three most important things in real estate are location, location, location." There is no substitute for being located in a central, aesthetically pleasing area that's close to easy-to-access transportation. (For residential real estate, other location pluses include proximity to a wide array of good retail options and access to a top-rated school district.)

A few other things affect value as well. Real estate in good repair is more valuable than a "fixer-upper." Some properties have intrinsic aesthetic value or history – this adds to their value. Basic macroeconomic factors also play a major role in the market. If interest rates are low, people rush to buy and refinance homes because of the attractive financing costs. And if demand is greater than supply, property prices rise.

Valuing real estate

There are three generally accepted approaches to valuing real estate: the sales approach, the cost approach and the income approach. Professional appraisers will reach a valuation after carefully considering each approach. You should make sure to review all three approaches before any real estate interview.

The sales approach

The sales approach arrives at a value for a property based on recent sales of similar properties. This approach can be used for both residential and commercial properties. There are proprietary databases that track home and commercial building sales, which make it easier for real estate professionals to access market information used in valuing properties. One of the most popular databases is the Multi-listing Service (MLS), which is used to track residential properties. The MLS contains useful information about homes, such as the sales history, tax records and property amenities that can be accessed for an annual fee. In the sales approach, appraisers will use databases, such as the MLS,

Visit Vault at www.vault.com for insider company profiles, expert advice, career message boards, expert resume reviews, the Vault Job Board and more.

VAULT CAREER LIBRARY

9

to look for homes with similar characteristics (e.g. location and house specifics), as the subject property. For example, when valuing a four-bedroom, two-bathroom house in the Pacific Heights section of San Francisco, it is logical to value that property based on the most recent sales information for properties in the same area with similar characteristics. Bear in mind that no two properties are alike, so when valuing a property using the sales approach you must adjust for differences between the properties.

The cost approach

In markets where it is difficult to find similar properties, an appraiser can value a property based on the cost approach. This approach focuses on a few steps. First, you must determine the cost of replacing or reconstructing the improvements or building. Next, the age of the improvements must be considered and an appropriate amount of depreciation is subtracted from the value of improvements. Finally, the value of the land must be taken into consideration. The land value is added to the improvements minus the estimated property depreciation. The cost approach is used for truly unique properties like churches, which cannot use either the sales or income approach to arrive at a valuation.

The income approach

The income approach is the most quantitative of the three approaches. The income approach involves the use of net operating income (NOI) in calculating the value of the property. (See the Appendix for a detailed explanation of Net Operating Income.) Think of NOI as the reason most investors buy a building. The investment community talks about NOI incessantly, so make sure to understand this concept if you plan on being involved with real estate investing.

There are two forms of the income approach. One form involves isolating NOI for one year, while the other form involves a longer time horizon. Both forms use a capitalization (cap) rate to calculate a value. The cap rate is a market mechanism, so don't worry about what goes in the calculation. Just be concerned with how it is used. In practice the cap rate is generally used in a formula with the NOI to arrive at a property value. For example, suppose you were buying an industrial facility whose net operating income in the following year was projected to be $500,000. If you knew the market cap rate for similar properties, you could arrive an estimated value of the property. Assume the market cap rate for industrial facilities was 10 percent. To arrive at the value of the building, divide NOI by the cap rate. In our example, the value of the building would be:

$$\text{Value} = \frac{\text{NOI}}{\text{Cap Rate}} = \frac{\$500,000}{.10} = \$5,000,000$$

The yield capitalization form uses a longer time horizon. It involves calculating a discounted cash flow to arrive a property value.

$$\text{Value} = \frac{\text{NOI year n}}{(1+\text{discount rate})^n} + \frac{\text{NOI year n}+1}{(1+\text{discount rate})^{n+1}} + \frac{\text{residual value}}{(1+\text{discount rate})^{n+1}}$$

In the example above, the numerator represents the cash flows that the building generates today and in the coming years, which theoretically provides a value for the asset. Note, that there is also a future residual value listed in the formula. The discount rate reflects the cost of capital. Your client may provide this cost, or you may have to estimate the discount rate based on similar transactions and knowledge of the market. The discount rate is necessary because it allows you to bring all the future cash flows back to today's dollars or present value (PV). The discount rate factors in the opportunity cost of money or the return that you could expect elsewhere with the cash flows. The exponent "n" in the denominator represents the period or number of years in the future that you would receive that cash flow. The DCF is calculated based on a stated number of years and adds up the PVs. At some point in the future cash flows you have a residual value because it is assumed the property is eventually sold. The residual value is calculated by taking the NOI of the year after the assumed time horizon and then dividing that year's NOI by an assumed cap rate. Some investors use different time periods when calculating the DCF but 10 years is the generally accepted period to value an asset. The DCF is normally used for income-producing property, while a single-family house is typically valued by the sales comparison approach.

Although there are different ways to value real estate, there are a few common variables such as location, the property's condition and market demand that make real estate valuable regardless of the asset type. There is a popular industry saying, "The three most important things in real estate are location, location, location." You simply cannot underestimate the importance of location. While you can restore and upgrade a property as much as you want, there is no substitute for being located close to: transportation, good schools, attractive retail and an aesthetically pleasing area. While location is important, keeping the property in good working order also creates value because it lessens the

Visit Vault at **www.vault.com** for insider company profiles, expert advice, career message boards, expert resume reviews, the Vault Job Board and more.

VAULT CAREER LIBRARY

11

need to make improvements or contribute capital to the property.   In addition, fundamental macroeconomics plays a major role in real estate values. For example, when interest rates offered by lenders are low, people will rush to buy a house to take advantage of the low financing costs. If this new market demand is greater than the market supply, property prices will increase.

Understanding Real Estate Finance

Generally speaking, real estate finance can be divided into equity and debt. You've probably heard the expression "down payment" in the context of buying a house. The down payment is usually the equity contribution or amount of capital that a buyer will supply toward the property purchase. For example, if you put $20,000 down on a house that costs $100,000 you now have 20 percent equity, or ownership, in the house and you will have to borrow the $80,000 balance, which represents the debt or the loan amount.

When the real estate involved is a more sophisticated asset, like an office building or a high-rise apartment, there may be multiple equity contributors.

There are many institutions that lend money (or "supply debt"). One of the more common lenders is a bank. The bank will lend money in return for principal and interest payments on the debt. Keeping with our example, assume the bank will lend the $80,000 needed to buy the house in return for 8 percent interest for 30 years. These debt payments, also called mortgage payments, include a principal portion and the interest portion. In our example, the principal portion is the $80,000 needed to buy the house and the interest portion is the amount that the bank charges the lender to borrow its $80,000. Over time, the buyer pays back the $80,000 and builds additional equity or ownership in the house.

Banks offer many different types of loans with different rates of interest and payback periods. Interest rates vary according to the associated risk and term. Loan products with the interest rate and accompanying term are published in *The Wall Street Journal* and the business section of most papers. Every lender has different criteria for its loans – e.g., some banks require buyers to put down at least 20 percent of the purchase price of the house, while others are more flexible. Banks perform a thorough background check on the borrower and the property.

If the borrower cannot make the principal and interest payments, the bank holds the house as collateral and ultimately may have to foreclose upon, or take back, the property. During a foreclosure, the borrower is essentially relieved of all rights to the property. This may be difficult for some people to accept, but the reality is that as it typically supplies most of the money, the bank retains protective provisions in case the borrower does not uphold his or her end of the bargain.

The preceding example involved a house, but the concept of equity and debt introduced is also applicable to buying an office building, hotel or warehouse erty. In principle, real estate sponsorship is no different than other forms of finance – lenders expect to be repaid and compensated for risk, while those who contribute equity are not guaranteed a return on their investment.

Mortgage Brokers

Companies or individuals hire a mortgage broker to find the best financing fit for the mortgage transaction. The transaction could involve a property purchase or refinancing assets that the client already owns. Mortgage brokers, intermediaries between real estate buyers and lenders, are valuable resources throughout the lending negotiations. They use a network of banks and other real estate lenders to find the best financing deal for their clients, often this means finding the most cost-effective loan.

If you want to find out more about this field, visit the National Association of Mortgage Brokers' web site (www.namb.org).

Calculating Mortgages

Most lenders and residential real estate brokers post easy-to-use mortgage calculators on their web sites. Additionally, Microsoft's Excel and most Hewlett Packard have a mortgage calculation feature. The calculators are a great resource for projecting potential mortgage payments.

Visit Vault at **www.vault.com** for insider company profiles, expert advice, career message boards, expert resume reviews, the Vault Job Board and more.

VAULT CAREER LIBRARY   13

Segmenting the Market

Real estate can be divided in two categories: residential and commercial. The home is the centerpiece of residential real estate, whereas commercial real estate is comprised of the office, apartment, hotel, industrial and retail sectors. Office buildings are the centerpieces of the office sector; apartment buildings are the focus of the apartment sector; traditional hotels and resorts make up the hotel sector; and stores and shopping centers are the centerpieces of the retail sector. Industrial real estate revolves around manufacturing facilities. The industrial category also includes storage and distribution facilities, as well as research and development facilities.

No matter what sector you're in, real estate is usually discussed in terms of square feet. For example, the price to lease or buy real estate is usually based on an annualized square foot basis.

Example: Company X occupies 10,000 square feet of space and pays an annual rent of $500,000. This rent translates into $50 per square foot – the annual rent divided by the total square feet. Almost every market adheres to this practice of calculating rent payments. California, one of the exceptions, calculates per square foot payments on a monthly basis. So, the $50 per square foot rate is divided by 12 and quoted as $4.17 per square foot per month.

Classification

The following section focuses on commercial real estate because residential relies less on a formal classification system and more on amenities (e.g., number of bedrooms and baths).

Since each commercial real estate asset is different, classification systems were created to label commercial real estate properties. If you plan on working in commercial real estate, you will need to become familiar with this terminology. While architectural significance plays a role in the classification, other characteristics such as location, construction quality, amenities, and technology infrastructure are the main drivers behind · classification.

Office buildings

Office buildings use a system of "classes" that range from A to D, where A is highest quality and D is lowest. There is a direct correlation between property classification and the cost to lease space – rents are higher per square foot in A properties and lower in D properties. Class A properties, sometimes called "trophy" buildings, typically have excellent access to transportation, state-of-the-art technology, high end finishes, contemporary design, strong management and additional amenities such as fitness facilities, white tablecloth restaurants, parking and convenient stores. Class B properties have good locations and solid management but typically display lesser quality construction and fewer amenities. Class C properties are dated buildings with a noticeable lack of upkeep and amenities. Class D properties are older buildings in sore need of renovation.

Retail real estate

Retail space consists of shopping malls, stand-alone tenants like Home Depot and mom and pop stores such as the local dry cleaners. There are three types of retail product: shopping centers, strip commercial and freestanding stores.

Shopping centers have their own subclassifications. Note that often you will hear the phrase "anchor tenant" in retail, which usually refers to the largest tenant at the mall.

- **Super regional centers** are the biggest of the big retail centers. The famed Mall of America in Minneapolis and the Galleria in Houston fall into this category. Super regional centers have three or more major department stores and draw customers from 12 miles or more. These malls are massive, at least 750,000 square feet in most cases.

- A **regional center** has at least one major department store, sometimes two, and an assortment of smaller stores. These malls are usually 300,000 square feet or larger.

- A **community center** has a smaller-sized department store and variety stores. Community center shopping centers are larger than 100,000 square feet and draw from a three- to five-mile radius.

- A **neighborhood center** has a supermarket or drugstore as an anchor tenant with other retail that provides goods and services to the community. These malls will draw from a one- to three-mile radius.

- **Convenience centers** are a collection of small stores that serve the immediate area. These centers range from 5,000-40,000 square feet.

- A **specialty** center is a facility meant for a specific narrow purpose, such as auto service and sales.

Visit Vault at **www.vault.com** for insider company profiles, expert advice, career message boards, expert resume reviews, the Vault Job Board and more.

VAULT CAREER LIBRARY   **15**

- **Big box stores** are meant for one user and are located near major shopping centers and along major thoroughfares. A tenant like Home Depot or Costco that serves a specific need would occupy these buildings.

- **Strip commercial** refers to a collection of smaller stores with no leasing, management or theme. Finally, freestanding stores are meant for one user and are located near major shopping centers and along major thoroughfares. You may also hear them referred to as "big box: retail. A tenant like Home Depot or Costco that serves a specific need would occupy these buildings.

Industrial real estate

Industrial buildings are generally not as aesthetically pleasing as other buildings, yet they are critical to the production process of many of items society on a daily basis. Industrial buildings have a wide variety of uses: research and development, manufacturing, transporting and warehousing. They differ from other real estate properties in a few distinct ways. For example, ceilings are often quite high because of the space requirements for equipment and storage racks. (When industrial space is converted to residential loft space, the high ceilings are often an attractive feature for many potential residents.) The height (of ceilings) is also sometimes called "clear." Industrial property must also have access to sufficient power to run any machinery on site.

Industrial properties also use a subclassification system.

- **Heavy industrial** properties are used for manufacturing purposes like auto making and material handling.

- **Warehouse and distribution** properties are used for storage purposes.

- **Light assembly** properties have limited manufacturing and focus on assembly of parts manufactured elsewhere.

- **Research and development (R & D)** facilities often have a combination of uses and are commonly used by biotech and product development firms. They may be a combination of research labs, traditional office space or storage.

Real Estate Investors

Real estate investing has become more sophisticated over the years and, like other ventures, there are both private and public markets. Anyone with sufficient capital can buy a house, office building, shopping center or industrial building as a private investor. However, if you don't have enough money or you prefer to spread the risk of ownership among a group of people and properties, you can buy shares in a real estate investment trust (REIT). REITs are an efficient way for sponsors to invest in the commercial and residential real estate businesses. As assets, they combine the best features of real estate and stocks, giving investors a practical and effective means to include professionally managed property in a diversified investment portfolio.

REITs were created by Congress in 1960 in an effort to allow small patrons to make investments in more sophisticated, income-producing real estate. The government believed that the average investor could only access these sophisticated properties through pooling vehicles. Consequently, REITs were designed to pool the capital of multiple investors into a single entity dedicated to real estate investment.

They were anything but an overnight sensation. REITs had to adhere to certain restrictions; initially they were allowed to own property but not manage it. This kept Wall Street money away because investors didn't like the idea of having third parties managing the assets. Nonetheless, REITs experienced a period of growth in the early 1970s until a recession hit in the middle of the decade.

The REIT market was relatively quiet until the late 1980s, when a series of events changed the marketplace. The Tax Reform Act of 1986 had a major impact, enabling REITs to operate and manage most types of income-producing commercial properties. The act also eliminated tax-motivated "paper losses" through depreciation deductions for most individual investors. This removal of real estate's tax-favored status, combined with the effect of the savings and loan crisis as well as overbuilding, led to a real estate slump in the late 1980s.

Ironically, REITs benefited from the dip in the real estate economy for two reasons. First, more REITs were formed than ever before. This growth was due to many private real estate companies struggling to survive in an environment where raising capital was difficult. Forming a REIT allowed access to public capital. Second, many investors were gambling on the real

Visit Vault at **www.vault.com** for insider company profiles, expert advice, career message boards, expert resume reviews, the Vault Job Board and more.

VAULT CAREER LIBRARY   17

estate market. They thought the real estate market had bottomed out and wanted to get on board before the market rebounded.

The modern REIT

Domestic REITs have exploded over the past 10 to 15 years. Today, there are over 300 REITs with over $300 billion in combined assets. REITs own roughly a third of commercial investment properties in the United States. Although most are public, there are also many private REITs. Like stocks, public REITs are traded on the major exchanges and have historically performed on par with other major indices like the Russell 2000 and S & P 500. They're available on every major exchange and many are included in mutual fund offerings. REITs invest in all types of real estate (e.g. hotels, malls, office buildings, even trailer parks!) directly through property purchases or mortgages.

REITs are run like most other public companies, with corporate officers and a board of directors who answer to stakeholders. Management makes decisions on which properties to buy and to sell and the directors often have ownership positions themselves. REITS can also be regional, national or international in focus.

Defining REITs

There are three main types of REITs: equity, mortgage and hybrid.

- **Equity REITs** develop, manage and invest in and own properties. Revenue from equity REITs comes principally from the rents charged in the buildings owned by the REITs.

- **Mortgage REITs** center around property mortgages. These REITs loan money to people or companies that buy real estate. Mortgage REITs also purchase existing mortgages or mortgage-backed securities. Instead of owning property, they generate their revenue from interest on these loans.

- **Hybrid REITs** invest in both properties and mortgages. They have the characteristics of both equity and mortgage REITs, hence the name.

In principle, the main benefits of REITs are liquidity for the real estate investor and a single level of taxation. Unlike most corporations, REITs are not taxed on the dividends paid to shareholders. The drawback with this practice is that since virtually all earnings are paid to shareholders, there is a limited amount of available cash left over. Therefore, REITs must constantly pursue capital for operations.

REITs have transformed the real estate industry and will continue to evolve. Before them, the industry lacked liquidity and values were less transparent. Now they're subject to complex tax laws and like other public companies, public REITs are bound by SEC guidelines.

In order for a corporation or trust to qualify as a REIT, it must comply with certain provisions within the Internal Revenue Code. As required by the Tax Code, a REIT must:

- Be a corporation, business trust or similar association.

- Be managed by a board of directors or trustees.

- Have shares that are fully transferable.

- Have a minimum of 100 shareholders.

- Have no more than 50 percent of the shares held by five or fewer individuals during the last half of each taxable year.

- Invest at least 75 percent of the total assets in real estate assets.

- Derive at least 75 percent of gross income from rents, real property or interest on mortgages on real property.

- Derive no more than 30 percent of gross income from the sale of real property held for less than four years, securities held for less than one year or certain prohibited transactions.

- Pay dividends of at least 95 percent of REIT taxable income.

For more information visit the National Association of REITs at www.nareit.org or call them at 800-3-NAREIT. Additionally, analysts are a great resource, such as Green Street Advisors (www.greenstreetadvisors.com), which is devoted to tracking REIT performance. The chart on the next page lists some of the higher profile REITs.

Visit Vault at www.vault.com for insider company profiles, expert advice, career message boards, expert resume reviews, the Vault Job Board and more.

VAULT CAREER LIBRARY   19

Major REITS

COMPANY	PROPERTY FOCUS	WEB SITE
EQUITY OFFICE PROPERITES	Office	www.equityoffice.com
EQUITY OFFICE RESIDENTIAL	Apartment	www.eqr.com
AMB	Industrial	www.amb.com
DUKE REALTY	Mixed	www.dukerealty.com
BOSTON PROPERTIES	Office	www.bostonproperties.com
GENERAL GROWTH PROPERTIES	Regional Malls	www.generalgrowth.com

Non-REIT Real Estate Investors

- **Pension funds** are also active investors in real estate. Almost any large pension fund will invest a portion of its assets in real estate as a means of diversifying its portfolio. Some are very sophisticated real estate investors; among the better known and active are California Public Employees' Retirement System (CalPERS), Teachers Insurance and Annuity Association (TIAA-CREF) and General Motors' pension fund.

- **Life insurance companies** have a long history of real estate investment. Like pension funds, they diversify a portion of their investment portfolio in real estate. There's a good chance that your insurance company invests in real estate – either lending or investing in property-related projects. National insurance giants like Allstate, Northwestern Mutual Life, Metropolitan Life and Prudential are all active real estate investors.

- **Opportunity funds** tend to invest in riskier transactions or assets and expect a high yield in return. They're extremely sophisticated and tend to be very analytical. Some of the prominent funds are affiliated with Wall Street banks like Goldman Sachs, Morgan Stanley and JP Morgan.

ON THE JOB

Real Estate Job Search Basics

CHAPTER 4

Unconventional Recruiting

Two things set real estate apart from other industries when it comes to hiring practices. The first is the lack of conventional recruiting. The second is the focus on personality. Real estate companies typically don't head to campuses or job fairs to recruit undergraduates and graduates, nor do they post openings on job boards. In fact, in a survey of real estate companies by Equinox Partners in October 2002, a paltry 17.9 percent of new hires in 2002 were recent graduates of real estate or MBA programs, according to a survey by Equinox Partners. The job market is opening up a bit, but most firms still rely on personal relationships to fill openings.

Leslie Boudreaux, a recruiter at Kforce who has placed candidates in the real estate industry, advises, "Our real estate clients look for a someone with three traits: a Rolodex, quantitative experience and excellent interpersonal skills. The Rolodex is necessary because you will be expected to access your network to get deals done. Quantitative experience is important because real estate companies do not want to train someone. Therefore, they look for someone who already has proven himself quantitatively – ideally, at a competitor. Finally, the person should be polished, intelligent, gregarious and sharp." She adds, "Overall, I would say the bulk of hiring within the industry is word of mouth, so individuals looking for work should reach out to as many people in the industry as possible."

Since most companies don't follow conventional recruiting processes, you need to be aggressive in your job search. There are opportunities. Just be prepared to do a lot of networking to uncover them.

A networking plan

Create a plan of attack to get the job you want. First, learn as much as you can about the company or companies of your choice, as well as the local real estate market. The best way to get a handle on the market, frankly, is to read local business publications, as real estate markets, by definition, are quite localized. Some of these publications include job listings but at the very least, you'll get a grasp on the major players in your local market; some of these publications include job listings as well. Some good web sites, such as

Globe Street (www.globest.com), also offer market-specific information. *(See the Appendix for a listing of other helpful web sites.)*

Undergraduates who are interested in real estate should take advantage of resources available on campus. Many universities offer real estate concentrations and classes and may even have a real estate club. This is a great introduction to the industry and will make you attractive to employers. If your campus has no real estate activities, take a few accounting and finance classes; firm grasp on fundamental finance concepts is essential to a career in the real estate industry.

Education

One possible educational route into real estate is to get an MBA at an institution with a specific real estate program. Some of the best programs, based on *U.S. News and World Report* rankings, are Wharton, University of California-Berkeley's Haas Business School, MIT's Sloan School of Management, University of Wisconsin-Madison and Ohio State University's Fisher School of Business. These schools also have strong real estate clubs that produce annual conferences and other activities.

Jobseeking Advice from a Real Estate Professor

Joseph Pagliari, a clinical assistant professor and director of the Real Estate Center at the Kellogg School of Management, says, "There are host of opportunities in real estate for MBAs. The issue is identifying the best fit for the candidate. Positions that are good fits for MBAs are with firms that supply capital to the industry. Typically these are large, sophisticated, financially-oriented firms. MBAs should identify these institutions and aggressively pursue them for employment. In today's marketplace, this means looking at REITs, mezzanine funds (funds built around mezzanine financing, which combines equity and fixed income investments) and private equity firms.

"In general the high profile real estate positions and financially rewarding jobs are on the capital side," adds Pagliari, who is also a principal of a real estate investment firm. "These jobs are almost self-selecting because they are tough to get and you have to be smart and aggressive to succeed. Given that positions in the capital side of the business are reserved for the elite, MBAs should pursue these positions because many of them possess the necessary qualities for these roles."

Employers look for a variety of skill sets. "It is difficult to narrow it to just a few things," he says. "Some positions are very quantitative while others emphasize strong interpersonal skills. Having a combination of both is a competitive advantage. In general, I tell all my students to look for roles that speak to their skill sets. It is going to be hard enough to get the interview, so don't blow it by going after a job that probably doesn't fit your background. MBAs should do their homework on the types of roles out there and match your background and interest with the best fit. However, you still want to shoot for the sky and leverage your MBA."

Job seekers shouldn't be shy about using their contacts "This industry is very tough for outsiders or newcomers to break into and students should be ready to accept that," he advises. "Get in the hunt as soon as possible and network, network, network. Using alums or anyone else you know in the industry is something I always recommend." When you have the interview, be prepared to talk about the local market – or any other in which the company operates. If it's a public firm, check *The Wall Street Journal* for the scuttlebutt. Also, be certain they'll welcome your MBA.

"In the interview you will most likely be asked about why you are interested in real estate and a few technical questions," Pagliari warns. "Be ready to describe a cap rate and market specifics like rental rates and general economic conditions."

To MBA students just starting a real estate program who know they want to enter the industry, he stresses, "Don't rely on simply taking real estate classes, especially if you have no prior real estate experience." You need to demonstrate passion by joining a real estate club or getting active in real estate-related activities at school. "Do whatever it takes to be able to demonstrate your enthusiasm for the industry," he adds. "If it takes starting a real estate club or being the driving force behind an event, then so be it."

The professor also advises individuals who are evaluating MBA programs that offer real estate curriculums to: make sure the professors have some practical experience and the curriculum will give you a skill set that will meet your end goal. Don't sacrifice the overall MBA experience for a school that simply offers a strong real estate curriculum and is lacking in other areas.

Visit Vault at **www.vault.com** for insider company profiles, expert advice,
career message boards, expert resume reviews, the Vault Job Board and more.

VAULT CAREER LIBRARY

25

For MBA students who are interested in real estate but whose programs do not offer real estate classes, Pagliari offers a solution. "Classes related to finance and economic principles that help you price risks are very useful," he says, noting that the ability to price risk is a strong differentiating factor. Pagliari also recommends taking business law classes because there are many legal issues involved in the industry. "Which is why you should not be surprised to find so many attorneys in the business," he says.

"I was a career switcher and was repeatedly asked in interviews about why I was interested in real estate," says Rich Monopoli, a recent graduate from business school. "Many of the interviewers wanted an explanation of how my background tied to my interest in real estate. I can't emphasize enough how important it is to be prepared to answer the question of why you are interested in real estate."

Job Hunting For Career Changers

If attending a specialized undergraduate or MBA program isn't an option, you'll have to work harder to develop your qualifications. The first step: get your real estate salesperson license. Pursuing your license will demonstrate your interest in the field and will expose you to real estate principles – it's neither terribly expensive nor time consuming.

You should also read and learn as much as possible about the industry. One great way to do this is to pick up one of the local periodicals that cover real estate. In New York, professionals read *Crain's*, *Commercial Property News* and *Real Estate Alert*. In Chicago, some of the more popular publications are *Crain's*, *Illinois Realtor* and *Midwest Real Estate News*. In Los Angeles, favorites include the *Los Angeles Business Journal* and *Southern California Real Estate Journal*. On a national level, *The Wall Street Journal* publishes a real estate report in every Wednesday's edition, that everybody in the real estate industry reads (or should).

One thing all undergraduates, MBAs and career switchers looking for positions in the industry should do is contact alumni from their schools who are active in real estate. A lot of schools do a great job of segmenting alumni by industry. In fact, some schools, like the University of Wisconsin and the University of Texas, publish a real estate alumni directory. Reaching out to alumni is very effective, and made all the more necessary because of the lack of formal recruiting. Many people in the business find their jobs through networking. Don't be shy! The real estate industry rewards the bold.

Once you get an interview, you must be prepared to turn on the charm. "Fit" with the company culture is vital, regardless of the specific position. Interpersonal skills are used in almost every facet of real estate, and interviewers will look for evidence of your charm and articulateness. Make sure you're relaxed and confident.

What to Expect

Over five million people in the United States work in real estate fields such as construction, mortgage banking, property management, real estate appraisals, brokerage and leasing and development. In addition, many others are engaged in corporate property and in real estate lending in commercial banks, savings and loans and insurance companies.

Real estate companies tend to be lean and keep overhead low. That means entry-level salaries are low; in many cases, they're based on commission. However, if you prove yourself, there are few industries that ultimately pay as well.

Although careers in real estate are varied, there are some common qualities that will help you succeed. Industry professionals are often entrepreneurial by nature and attentive to detail. Employers will take note if you're analytical, creative and charismatic as well as a good negotiator.

You may also want to contact a recruiter that specializes in real estate to get some additional ideas. Two top recruiting firms are Whitney Group (on the Web at www.whitneygroup.com) and the Advisory Group (found at www.fplassociates.com.)

Getting a Real Estate Scholarship

Did you know there are scholarships offered by professional real estate organizations? For example, PREA, or the Pension Real Estate Association, offers a scholarship to students. Getting money for school is great, of course, but perhaps even more valuable is the opportunity to list the scholarship on your resume. See PREA.org for more information.

Visit Vault at **www.vault.com** for insider company profiles, expert advice, career message boards, expert resume reviews, the Vault Job Board and more.

V/\ULT CAREER LIBRARY   27

Use the Internet's
MOST TARGETED
job search tools.

Vault Job Board

Target your search by industry, function, and experience level, and find the job openings that you want.

VaultMatch Resume Database

Vault takes match-making to the next level: post your resume and customize your search by industry, function, experience and more. We'll match job listings with your interests and criteria and e-mail them directly to your inbox.

> VAULT
> the most trusted name in career information™

Residential Real Estate Agents/Brokers

CHAPTER 5

The Scoop

Residential real estate agents help buyers and sellers in the process of selling or renting residential property. Some agents work with buyers, helping them find places to live and negotiating with sellers. Other agents work with the sellers. Agents rarely represent both buyers and sellers, since this is perceived as a conflict of interest. For property rentals, almost all agents represent property owners. There are close to 500,000 real estate brokers and agents in the United States.

Agents are usually independent sales professionals who contract their services to sponsoring real estate brokers in exchange for a commission-sharing agreement. The commission on a home sale varies by market but is roughly five to six percent of the sale price. This commission is split four ways among the seller's agent, buyer's agent and the sponsoring brokers with whom each agent is associated. Many agents work solely on commission and don't get much in the way of benefits. Agents are expected to cover most of the overhead necessary to perform their jobs.

In order to sell real estate services, you must be a licensed professional in the state where you do business. To become a realtor, all states require that you pass a written exam focused on real estate law and transactions and be affiliated with a broker. Most states require you to be at least 18 years old and a high school graduate, and to have completed a minimum number of classroom hours. Some states waive the classroom requirements for active attorneys or offer correspondence course credit options in lieu of the classroom hour requirement. The license fee depends on the state, but expect to pay around $100 for the exam and $400 for the classes.

Although there are different organizations through which you can receive your classroom instruction, the state government issues and oversees licenses. If you visit the National Association of Realtor's web site at www.realtor.org, you can find information about residential real estate as well as licensing requirements for each state and locations of authorized real estate classes.

This industry attracts all types of personalities. There's a potpourri of career switchers, from lawyers to housewives, who end up in residential real estate.

Visit Vault at **www.vault.com** for insider company profiles, expert advice, career message boards, expert resume reviews, the Vault Job Board and more.

VAULT CAREER LIBRARY   29

If you like being your own boss and interacting with people, being a realtor can be very rewarding.

On the Job

Real estate agents generally focus on buying and selling (or renting) homes or land for building residential developments on behalf of another party. The job involves matching a client's home wish list with with houses available in the marketplace, or to sell the client's house in a timely manner at his or her asking price. Agents make most of their paycheck from commissions.

To be a good agent you need a thick skin, strong interpersonal/networking skills and a good sense of finance. The need to find clients and properties to sell or rent through cold calls, constant schmoozing and mass mailings tends to discourage some from residential realty.

Hours are flexible – to a point. Many people like to househunt after work or on weekends, so if you cherish those times, this job isn't for you. Also, because you're not on a set schedule, you need to be disciplined about getting your work done.

You should have at least a basic knack for figures and calculation – you'll be working with a variety of budgets, mortgage rates and other figures. If you're not a math whiz, don't worry: While it helps to be analytical, it's much more important to be dedicated, organized and have a talent for schmoozing.

The workday

If you're sick of being held to a schedule, then residential real estate may be the field for you. You set your own hours, and have no need to stop into the office except to file paperwork or maybe for the occasional staff meeting. At the same time, your time may not be as flexible as you might imagine. Open houses – when a property for sale is shown to the general public – are invariably held on evenings or weekends. Your clients may be unable to see properties during the traditional workweek as well.

Residential real estate agents are responsible for a variety of tasks. Some days are reserved for marketing homes for sale. Others are spent making networking calls and advertising for new clients. Even after a sales contract is signed, the work of the agent is not done. Agents must organize a final home inspection prior to closing, to make sure that the home is in good working order and that all the work the buyer asked to be done prior to the closing has, in fact, been done. Agents must communicate between the buyer and the seller to make sure all this work occurs in a timely and orderly fashion.

Training

If you're looking to residential realty for thorough training, you're going to be disappointed. Only the largest residential real estate brokers offer formal training programs. For everyone else, training comes on the job. To pick up the tools of the trade, "be aggressive about asking questions and shadowing senior agents," suggests Nellie MacDiarmid McCarthy, a licensed sales agent with Century 21 Sussex and Reilly in Chicago. "Developing a relationship with a mentor is one of the better ways to learn. Shadow him or her at open houses and showings."

As you become more senior, the only changes in your day-to-day role may be management responsibility and/or mentoring a new agent. Essentially, the job will stay the same. The top dogs in the business get a lot of name recognition and perks from their brokers. At this point, you'll have business come to you because your name is so well known. Many top agents invest in real estate themselves; some agents leave their brokers to start their own agencies.

On the one hand, residential real estate is an exquisitely flexible field. Realtors can set their own hours, but to satisfy clients' scheduling needs, many find themselves working between 50 and 60 hours a week, especially when they are first learning the business and establishing themselves in the real estate community.

Good agents need to be organized, knowing enough about each phase of the buying and selling process to keep things moving smoothly (and legally). Handling clients is also vitally important. People get very emotional when buying or selling a house, and are often very nervous about the large sums of money spent or acquired. Because of these emotional factors, managing clients and their expectations is a crucial responsibility for the successful realtor.

Compensation

Since agents work on commission rather than on salary, it's difficult to predict compensation. The gross commission on the home sale is divided between the broker representing the seller and the broker representing the buyer. As mentioned before, the gross commission is roughly five or six percent of the sale price in most markets. The brokers then divide their shares with the agent(s) involved in the transaction.

Agents have different commission agreements with their sponsoring brokers (effectively, their employers). As a new agent, expect at least a 50/50 commission split with your broker. As the agent, you would expect to make half of the commission paid to your brokerage, while your sponsoring broker will collect the other half. As you gain seniority, you can negotiate for a higher commission split and other privileges. Many brokers have a tiered commission split in place based on volume. For example, a broker may pay better splits once an agent gets past $100,000 in gross commissions. Of course, this all depends on pre-negotiated agreements and company policy – so ask before you take that job!

One thing to consider is that it takes a while to start making money. "You can look at it in phases," McCarthy adds. "First you have to build your client base, then you have to wait for the closing. Hit the ground running hard and use your network of friends." Many realtors suggest you enter the profession with six months of savings to guard against the initial slow months.

Often there's a system in place so agents can pay their bills while they wait for commissions. Brokers will pay agents a draw, which is an interest free loan the broker expects to be repaid from the agent's commission. Draws are negotiable but are reconciled every quarter. If the agent falls too far behind in paying back the draw, the he or she will be expected to repay the draw or may even be released from the brokerage.

If you're good at this job and work full time, you can expect to make up to $80,000 in your first year and close to $100,000 as you gain experience. Remember that you're making a commission based on the sale price of the house. Average home prices will influence your commission. Therefore, if you're working in a market where homes are expensive you will make more money than if you sell the same amount of property in a less expensive market. Also, keep in mind agents are independent contractors and not employees, so they aren't entitled to benefits.

Getting Paid

Assume you are the agent representing the seller in a transaction where the house is sold for $1,000,000. Further assume that the gross sales commission was 5 percent, or $50,000, and will be split equally between your sponsoring broker and the broker representing the buyer. Therefore, each broker receives $25,000. From this point on we aren't concerned about the broker or the agent who represented the buyer in the transaction – just "your" $25,000.

Assume your pre-negotiated split arrangement with your sponsoring broker gives you 70 percent. So, the net commission of $25,000 will be split such that you receive $17,500 and the sponsoring broker gets $7,500. Not a bad payday! At this pace, though, the agent must average a closing every two months, or six a year, to make a six-figure income.

Getting Hired

There aren't many barriers to becoming a real estate agent, largely due to the minimal investment made on the part of the sponsoring broker. Essentially, you're given a desk and phone and left to your own devices to find potential buyers and sellers and learn other aspects of the business. It helps if you already have your license, but most brokers will let you on board with the understanding that you'll have one in the near future. Sometimes you can negotiate the cost of the class and exam into your hiring package. Be sure to ask in the interview if the sponsoring broker subsidizes the real estate exam fee.

Brokers look for energetic, self-confident and independent individuals. It will help your cause if you have a working idea of what's involved in buying or selling a home. Become familiar with how interest rates impact home buying, the health of the local real estate market and what it takes to get a mortgage. Also, heading into an interview with a business plan for acquiring clients should impress your potential sponsor. Honest people who possess strong marketing skills do well in this industry. Note that some brokers don't require you to have a college education, others do. It depends on the firm.

There's a lot of turnover in this business, so beware of potentially apathetic employers. Make sure they'll work with you to help you learn the business. Talk to other brokers at the company you are considering. Ask them candid questions about how the broker treats their agents; ask specifically about employee turnover. Ask is how the broker handles leads or referrals. Some brokers don't have a equitable system in place to distribute leads or referrals

Visit Vault at **www.vault.com** for insider company profiles, expert advice, career message boards, expert resume reviews, the Vault Job Board and more.

V/\ULT CAREER LIBRARY   **33**

to the sales agents, so only favored agents get business while everyone else is left to fend for himself. Finally, be sure to ask about reimbursable expenses. In the course of marketing properties or entertaining, you will be spending money, so you should ask the company about its reimbursement policy.

Questions to ask

- What kind of training do you offer?

- What are the commission splits?

- What is the average tenure of your agents?

- How do you distribute leads or referrals among agents?

- Will I be reimbursed for expenses related to my real estate license?

Questions to expect

- Do you have your license?

- How long are you prepared to work making no or very little money?

- Why do you want to be a real estate agent?

- How do you expect to find clients?

- How are your organization skills?

- How strong are your interpersonal skills?

A Day in the Life of a Residential Real Estate Agent

9:00 a.m.: Get in the office, check voice mail and e-mail. Create to-do list for the day.

9:30 a.m.: Place calls on behalf of a client looking to buy a house to set up a tour for this weekend. Ask the sellers' agent to fax over the property listing sheets that contain all the vital information on the house. Confirm the asking price and try to figure out if the property is in demand or determine the flexibility of the sellers.

10:15 a.m.: Check in with co-workers to find out what deals they are working on and if they have any market scoop (i.e., trade sale comparables).

11:00 a.m.: Lob a call to a client buyer's attorney to see if everything is going smoothly with a pending property purchase. Find out that items discovered on the property inspection are being addressed. Call client to relay the information and reassure her the closing will happen later that week as planned. Have a brief discussion about mortgage rates.

12:00 p.m.: Break for a lunch with a mortgage broker. Talk about what is happening with mortgage rates and receive thanks for all the referrals you've passed on to him.

1:30 p.m.: Check and return voice mail and e-mails. Organize marketing materials for delivery that day. Hand the deliverables to an administrative assistant to mail.

3:30 p.m.: Head to the title company to close a deal. Your client is the buyer. Huddle up with the attorney and the client to make sure everyone is happy. Everything runs smoothly. Get a cashier's check made out to the broker. Thank client and tactfully remind them to refer your services to their friends.

5:00 p.m.: Back to the office. Give the check to your manager and give self a pat on the back. Ask about timetable for payment of the commission and return to desk. A co-worker gives a high five.

5:30 p.m.: Check e-mail and voice mail one more time. Put out fires and check commissions for the past year to see how your sales compare to those of your co-workers.

6:00 p.m.: Make sure everything is set for your upcoming home tours. Open up prospect list, record the closed deal and see what deals you expect to close in the near future.

7:00 p.m.: End of the day. Co-worker who gave the high five reminds you that you promised to buy drinks once your deal closed.

Visit Vault at **www.vault.com** for insider company profiles, expert advice,
career message boards, expert resume reviews, the Vault Job Board and more.

VAULT CAREER LIBRARY   **35**

Losing sleep over your job search?
Endlessly revising your resume?
Facing a work-related dilemma?

Super-charge your career with Vault's newest career tools: Resume Reviews, Resume Writing and Career Coaching.

Vault Resume Writing

On average, a hiring manager weeds through 120 resumes for a single job opening. Let our experts write your resume from scratch to make sure it stands out.

- Start with an e-mailed history and 1- to 2-hour phone discussion
- Vault experts will create a first draft
- After feedback and discussion, Vault experts will deliver a final draft, ready for submission

Vault Resume Review

- Submit your resume online
- Receive an in-depth e-mailed critique with suggestions on revisions within TWO BUSINESS DAYS

Vault Career Coach

Whether you are facing a major career change or dealing with a workplace dilemma, our experts can help you make the most educated decision via telephone counseling sessions.

- Sessions are 45-minutes over the telephone

For more information go to
www.vault.com/careercoach

VAULT
> the most trusted name in career information™

Commercial Real Estate Brokerage –
Tenant Representation

CHAPTER 6

The Scoop

Commercial property brokerage offices employ sales associates who market office buildings, hotels and many other types of commercial real estate for third party interests. Commercial real estate sales people usually specialize in a particular property type, such as apartments, retail, office buildings, hotels, shopping centers or industrial buildings. Most of the large commercial brokerage companies in the U.S. produce a great deal of local market data and research in order to service sophisticated clients making multimillion-dollar investment decisions. Like residential agents, sales associates must be licensed and have a sponsoring broker to conduct transactions. The salesperson license a commercial broker holds is the same one residential agents use.

There are two types of commercial real estate sales associates: those who represent landlords and those who represent tenants. There is some overlap between the roles, but there are also key differences that you should consider before pursuing these careers. This chapter covers tenant representation; Chapter 7 covers work for the landlord.

On the Job

A tenant representation agent, commonly known as a "tenant rep," represents companies and other corporate clients looking to lease or buy either a portion of a property or an entire real estate asset. A large part of this job involves business development. Since tenant reps are often responsible for building their own book of business, prospecting for new clients is a big part of the job. Like residential agents, tenant reps are left to their own devices to find prospects. Although there's some direction by the broker and senior tenant reps in the office, for the most part you're cold-calling tenants or companies. First, you need to give the person on the other end of the phone a compelling reason to meet with you, then you must pitch the business. It's a tough sell.

Tenant representation is very competitive, even cutthroat. You're not only competing against outside reps but those inside your office. In fact, some tenant rep brokers think the competition inside is worse than outside the shops. Often there are disputes about who is entitled to chase what business.

Ultimately, the senior brokers tend to win. Deal protocol is important to consider when you're selecting brokers because often there are disputes are common among tenant reps.

When the time comes for one of his or her clients to buy, sell or lease, the tenant rep finds a list of choices in the market, then handles the accompanying negotiations. Tenant reps usually work in teams to spread the work. Often the team is composed of one senior and one junior broker. The junior broker will make the cold calls and set up meetings with prospective clients. At the meetings the senior broker will take the lead and try to win the business. Once the process begins, the junior broker will do the legwork for market alternatives and examine options with the senior broker. All possible alternatives are presented to the client for review. The senior broker generally handles the lease or sale negotiations. This mutually beneficial system gives the senior broker a "cold caller" and provides a training platform for the junior broker. Junior brokers should expect to work at least 50 to 60 hours per week; senior brokers' hours fluctuate based on deal flow.

Once junior brokers have surpassed certain earning requirements, they're promoted to senior brokers. They still make cold calls to get leads, though not nearly as often as junior brokers. The company relies on its senior brokers to win business and handle transactions from start to finish. Sometimes senior brokers help create and execute management policy and even have equity at smaller firms.

Compensation

Like residential agents, many commercial sales associates operate on commission and split commissions with the managing broker. (Some firms pay base salaries, but this practice is not common.) The commission structure differs based on property type and is determined by a formula more complex than the simple split used for residential brokers. This formula typically depends on seniority, base pay and the size of the transaction. For instance, the commission could be stated as $.80 per square foot per year. On a 10-year lease transaction for 10,000 square feet the gross commission calculation would be $.80 times 10,000 (square feet) times 10 (years) or $80,000. Not a bad payout. But wait a minute! This pie has yet to be split up. The tenant rep still has to give the managing broker his or her share and then split the rest among the team. At the end of the day, the split may look something like the following: you give 50 percent to the managing broker and split the remaining net amount with your teammate(s) evenly. In our example, that yields $20,000 each to the senior and junior broker. Note that the sales cycle is long, so it can take a while to get paid, sometimes as long as a year. The norm is that building owners pay half of the commission upon lease signing and the remainder when the tenant moves in.

Commissions vary by geography and product type, so the above example should not be considered representative of all areas. For example, the commission in New York may be higher than it would be in Washington, DC.

Tenant rep can be very rewarding, but does have its risks. Remember, no individual can control the economy. Some deals don't materialize. When the economy is in bad shape, companies are less active in the market and you may have few to no commissions! Your client may pull the plug on the deal at any time, leaving you with nothing for your time and hard work. Make no mistake about it, tenant reps are usually risktakers who like big payoffs.

Getting Hired

One major difference between residential agents and commercial brokers is the sophistication of the client. In commercial real estate you are calling on senior management – the CEO, CFO or COO of a company. These people are used to making major decisions and prefer to have a lot of information beforehand. Also, executives expect immediate answers to their questions.

Strong presentation skills and dependability are a must. If you are switching careers, it helps if you have a sales background. Expect to be asked why you're interested in real estate and why you'd be successful in sales. This field is similar in some ways to residential real estate sales, but harder to break into.

Commercial real estate is normally a less emotional transaction than residential; it is more of a business decision. If clients are dissatisfied with tenant reps, they find it easy to fire them. Unfortunately, this happens more than you might care to believe. The corporate community is small, however, so doing a good job for one senior manager will invariably lead to more business.

Questions to ask

- Is there a training program?

- Will I be expected to team up with a senior broker?

- How do you handle commission disputes among brokers?

Visit Vault at **www.vault.com** for insider company profiles, expert advice, career message boards, expert resume reviews, the Vault Job Board and more.

V/\ULT CAREER LIBRARY   **39**

- Do you restrict the areas or the companies that your brokers are allowed to call on?

- How many of the senior brokers started as junior brokers at this company?

- How long does it usually take to become a junior broker and what is the criteria for advancement?

Questions to ask

- Why are you interested in real estate?

- Why will you be successful in sales? (Be ready to demonstrate this with examples)

- How do you feel about making cold calls?

- Can you give me an example of a time you exhibited strong teamwork skills?

A Day in the Life of a Commercial Sales Agent

7:30 a.m.: Things usually start early. Get into the office, check voice mail and go through contact database to line up cold calls for the day. Scan the *Wall Street Journal* or the local paper's business section to see if clients, prospects or other relevant industry news are mentioned in the paper. Remind self about working on commission and motivate.

8:15 a.m.: Huddle up with partner to discuss to-dos. Perhaps discuss current lease or purchase negotiations and strategy. Divide tasks to be done and set up a team meeting time for the end of the day.

9:00 a.m.: Check in with some co-workers to find out what deals they're working on and if they have some market news (i.e., trade lease or sale comparables and find out which tenants are in the market).

9:30 a.m.: Start morning cold calls. Try to set up meetings with decision makers and find out as much as possible over the phone about their real estate needs. Determine who makes real estate decisions. Make note to follow up with marketing material later that day.

12:00 p.m.: Break for a pre-scheduled lunch with a client. (Sometimes you have lunch with prospective clients, leasing agents, or colleagues.) Discuss market conditions and try to extract information that will help get more business or help current lease negotiations.

1:30 p.m.: Check and return voice mail and e-mails.

2:30 p.m.: Check in with clients and clients' attorneys to discuss ongoing lease or purchase negotiations. Make calls to architects or contractors to see how your building is progressing. Report any time - sensitive information to client. Set up building tours for later in the week and try to get a sense what the owners of each building are looking for financially and how desperate they are for a deal.

4:00 p.m.: Write follow-up letters and prepare marketing material for prospects. Call internal accounting department to see when you will be receiving your outstanding commission checks. After explaining the time value of money to them, threaten them. Call back and apologize and beg. Perhaps now your checks will come in a timely fashion.

5:00 p.m.: Check in with your sales manager. She wants to know which deals will close this quarter and if everything is on track to hit forecasted numbers. Complain about the accounting department and pump her for information about where your sales numbers are in relation to your co-workers'.

5:30 p.m.: One last meeting with partner to recap the day. Discuss any problems and come up with solutions. Make follow-up phone calls together to leasing agents or clients. Gossip about the day's market activity. Set a meeting time for the next day.

6:15 p.m.: Finally get to your mail (in this business you get a lot). Receive a written response to a request for a proposal from a building. Make a copy for partner and review the details. Hand another copy to the analyst to run the numbers associated with the deal.

6:45 p.m.: End of the day. Contemplate whether or not to head to an industry function.

Visit Vault at **www.vault.com** for insider company profiles, expert advice,
career message boards, expert resume reviews, the Vault Job Board and more.

VAULT CAREER LIBRARY   41

For Further Reference

There are more large commercial brokers than residential brokers. Some well-known tenant rep companies are Julien J. Studley (www.studley.com), Cushman & Wakefield (www.cushwake.com), CB Richard Ellis (www.cbre.com) and Jones Lang LaSalle (www.joneslanglasalle.com).

Commercial Real Estate Brokerage –
Leasing Agent

CHAPTER 7

The Scoop

The leasing agent position is the flip side of commercial real estate brokerage – the complement to the tenant rep. These agenets lease space at a property for a third-party company, an owner or a REIT. The leasing agent is employed by the owner as an intermediary to show and lease vacant space and negotiate leases for existing tenants wanting to renew. Many owners expect monthly reports on tenants in the market for space, companies that have toured the building, competitive rents and explanations for why tenants chose another building instead of yours.

On the Job

A big part of the leasing agent position entails collecting as much information on the local market as possible and concisely conveying that data to the owner of the building. He or she relies on the agent to obtain a fair market lease as well as to represent ownership when showing the building. Consequently, the leasing agent has to know everything happening at the building and in the surrounding market. Leasing agents should also be familiar with the history of both. They should also be able to recite the names of every tenant residing in the building and when their leases expire. Good leasing agents are very organized and give thorough building tours.

Leasing agents must be social. Good agents are in regular contact with their tenants and carefully monitor lease expirations in their buildings. In order to get the market information you need, you must constantly network with your peers. Tenant reps are said to control 90-95 percent of the marketplace. That means good leasing agents form relationships with the top tenant reps. Leasing agents are generally given a budget for entertaining the brokerage community so they can effectively gather information on who's looking for space and market their company's buildings. Becasue of this, leasing agents can develop reputations as great party throwers and for their marketing creativity. While this is fun, some brokers tire of the entertaining, especially when it doesn't translate into deals.

Leasing agents often lease more than one building and, like tenant reps, sometimes work in teams. Additionally, there are some that moonlight as tenant rep brokers or act as consultants on building purchases. Some owners discourage this practice because of conflict of interest concerns.

The natural progression is to move from junior to senior leasing agent. The difference between these two roles is more leasing responsibility. Instead of representing just leasing one property, senior agents handle leasing for multiple buildings. They're also responsible for helping to win more business – securing leasing assignments from owners. Very successful leasing agents are generally opportunistic and, after being in the business for a while, develop a network of owners who prefer to work with them. They become familiar with which assets different owners look for and try to identify buildings that meet these criteria. If they identify an opportunity and the owner buys the building, they're entitled to a commission on the sale. The best agents sometimes receive equity in the company for which they work.

Compensation

Unlike tenant reps, leasing agents generally get a salary in addition to a performance-based commission. While this may not be as lucrative as tenant representation, there isn't as much emphasis on prospecting for clients. Although less risky than tenant representation, there's still unpredictability associated with this role. A good agent may potentially lease himself out of a job. Once the building is occupied, your responsibilities dwindle. Additionally, leasing contracts with owners are short-term (and void if the property is sold). Owners can be demanding and are constantly feeling out competing leasing companies. If, for whatever reason, you're removed from a building, you can only hope your company has another building for you to lease.

Getting Hired

Good tenant reps "must be extremely presentable, a multitasker and aggressive (in a tactful way)," advises Mitch Loveman, senior vice president at Transwestern Commercial Services. "You represent the building, so you must carry yourself very well. The good leasing agents know their building and their competition and have a strong working relationship with the real estate community."

Leasing agents must have a salesperson license. Most firms require a college education and an understanding of basic finance. Expect to be asked about your organizational and interpersonal skills. Furthermore, don't be surprised if you're asked market-specific questions relating to competitors, vacancy, lease rates and the owner's property portfolio. Be sure to ask about the property's marketing plan, how the leasing team interacts on a daily basis and career progression. Having prior sales experience can be a big plus. If you can demonstrate that you're comfortable presenting and that you are an effective communicator, you'll do well in this position.

Questions to expect

• Do you have your real estate salesperson's license?

• How much finance did you take in college?

• How much finance related work experience do you have?

• How are your organizational skills? Can you provide an example of a project you worked on that demonstrates strong organizational skills

• Are you comfortable making presentations? Do you have experience making presentations?

• What is the vacancy rate in _____? (Insert the market in which you interviewing.)

• What are market lease rates?

• Who do you consider my competitors?

Questions to ask

• What is your property/portfolio goal?

• Do you expect growth or contraction in your portfolio?

• What is your strategy to reach that goal?

• What is your property's competitive advantage?

• Please describe your current leasing team's structure, their responsibilities and how each team member interacts.

Visit Vault at **www.vault.com** for insider company profiles, expert advice, career message boards, expert resume reviews, the Vault Job Board and more.

VAULT CAREER LIBRARY   45

Investment Sales Broker

CHAPTER 8

The Scoop

The investment sales broker represents a real estate investor looking to buy, sell or finance a real estate asset. These brokers work with all real estate asset classes – apartments, office buildings, industrial, hotel and others. Investors hire these brokers to provide strategic advice, market knowledge and access to capital. Note that many owners, such as REITs, have their own acquisition and disposition groups and often handle this function in house rather than hire a third party.

Investment sales brokers deal with more complicated issues than residential or commercial brokers. The clients are very sophisticated and the finance involved can be complex. Brokers should understand how differing levels of equity and debt impact a purchase decision and the asset's return. For example, if the deal terms change and the buyer has to borrow more money than anticipated the additional mortgage payments may diminish the annual income the buyer had forecasted. Good investment sales brokers will work with the buyer to determine if there are additional financing vehicles available. Most of the people in this business have a balance of analytical and people skills, therefore, good investment brokers are personable and understand how analytical issues such as finance impact clients.

On the Job

Marketing makes up a large part of this business. Brokers are always pitching real estate investors for assignments. They identify opportunities by networking with investors and anyone else that may provide leads. They don't need to make as many cold calls as tenant reps, but still must be aggressive. Once a broker identifies an investor to represent, he must still convince the investor he's worthy of the assignment. This job involves making a lot of presentations to potential clients, entertaining investors, and endless number crunching. Typically, an owner interviews multiple brokers for an assignment. Like other brokers, they distinguish themselves with their market knowledge and their track record.

Once a broker gets an assignment, he needs to execute the sale, purchase or financing. The sale of an asset involves putting together detailed property information that will help an investor make an educated decision. The marketing materials include pictures of the property, financial analyses and information about the local market. In a property purchase, the broker helps the investor digest the marketing information and provides a frame of reference for similar transactions. The broker may have to determine which financial structure meets the investor's goals when the deal involves financing an asset.

Investment sales brokers tend to work in teams. Those new to the field come in as associates. The associate is the junior person on the team and is responsible for putting together marketing materials, generating financial analysis and any other paperwork linked to the deal. Above the associate is a vice president, who is expected to bring in business, supervise the transactions and handle the majority of client contact. The managing director heads the office and is the ultimate decision maker, responsible for managing all of the transactions as well as the office.

Compensation

Investment sales brokers are very high profile operators in the real estate industry and usually make attractive salaries. Although some do get paid a salary, most earn the bulk of their income from commissions. In today's market, the total commission is roughly two percent of the total sales price (e.g., a $100,000,000 sale has a gross commission of $2,000,000). Unlike residential real estate, the commission is not paid entirely by the seller. For example, in the sale of a large industrial park, the seller and the buyer may *each* pay their respective brokers one percent of the sale price. Commissions are split among the team and the company.

Getting Hired

Getting a job as an investment sales broker without prior real estate experience is difficult. You need to have a strong balance of quantitative and qualitative skills to help you win business, and these qualities are often the reason that candidates are hired. Most investors tend to be small and multitask, which makes it particularly difficult to break into the field. Expect to be asked how your background will benefit the team.

These brokers have a strong understanding of valuation. A candidate that has experience valuing assets has an edge. In an interview for an investment sales broker position, be prepared to answer questions about what investors look for in a property. Also be prepared to discuss the different asset classes in your local market, as well as recent sales information. Again, this is probably one of the more sophisticated parts of the business, so make sure you're extremely presentable in an interview.

If you know you want to be in the business, but don't have the requisite skill set, you can always start in another facet of the industry. For example, commercial brokers have been known to break into this field after establishing themselves as top performers.

If you feel you have the requisite skills to be an investment sales broker, contact some of the firms listed in this guide (see the Appendix) and be prepared to answer how you will add value to the team. Eastdil (www.eastdil.com) and Marcus & Millichap (www.marcusmillichap.com) are two respected investment brokers with offices across the country. Also, some full-service real estate firms have investment sales groups in major markets.

Questions to ask

• What is the background of the team members?

• What type of experience does the firm look for in a candidate?

• How does the investment team disseminate work?

Visit Vault at **www.vault.com** for insider company profiles, expert advice,
career message boards, expert resume reviews, the Vault Job Board and more.

V/\ULT CAREER LIBRARY   **49**

A Day in the Life of an Investment Sales Broker

8:00 a.m.: Start the day by checking your e-mail and voice mails. Next, start reading some of the industry standard periodicals. These include the Real Estate Alert, the local paper's business section and, of course, *The Wall Street Journal*.

8:45 a.m.: Check in with the associate to make sure the marketing literature and the financial analysis for a property sale will be ready after lunch. Go over some additional scenarios and ask him to include them in the financial analysis.

9:15 a.m.: Place a call to a local owner to discuss the possibility of selling his building. He asks for an opinion on what his property will fetch and about properties for sale that meet his investment criteria should he decide to buy another building. He also asks about options if he decides to refinance his property.

9:30 a.m.: Receive a call from a competitor requesting information about a property for sale. Realize he's reaching for information that the seller isn't prepared to disclose. Switch gears and ask him about his listings and the business he is chasing.

10:00 a.m.: The managing director swings by and asks for a memo updating a foreign client on the state of the domestic real estate market.

10:45 a.m.: Give the managing director the finished memo and get ready for a meeting in which the team will discuss strategy for a property purchase. The team discusses recent comparable sales, the condition of the property and a client's investment objectives.

12:30 p.m.: Break for lunch with a colleague or a competitor and discuss the market. There is a lot of discussion about the cost of capital for real estate assets and about the local estate market conditions.

2:00 p.m.: Check in with the associate and make sure marketing literature and financial analysis will get done today.

2:15 p.m.: Have a conference call with a client to discuss the status of a property purchase. The client is concerned about overpaying for the property. Assure him his offer is in line with market comparables and the property is worth the price.

3:00 p.m.: Review materials the associate prepared. After checking the documents, return e-mails and see how the financial markets did that day.

4:00 p.m.: A colleague from another city calls to discuss the condition of your local market. He has a client who may be interested in buying a property in the area and wants to discuss the possibility of partnering on the deal. Tell him you will speak with your managing director about it and get back to him.

4:30 p.m.: Drop in on the managing director to tell him about the partnering opportunity. He instructs you to negotiate the commission splits up front and make sure to get everything in writing.

5:00 p.m.: Direct the associate to package the marketing information and financial analysis for your property sale in a book, and send it out to a list of probable buyers.

5:15 p.m.: Hit the phones one last time to return phone calls, trying to catch some colleagues in another market where a client may be interested in buying real estate.

6:00 p.m.: End of the day. Realizing your deal flow is small, schedule a meeting for later that week with the team to discuss new business initiatives.

Visit Vault at **www.vault.com** for insider company profiles, expert advice, career message boards, expert resume reviews, the Vault Job Board and more.

VAULT CAREER LIBRARY   51

Mortgage-Backed Securities Rating Agencies

CHAPTER 9

The Scoop

Lenders or debt-holders, such as banks, sometimes accumulate a considerable amount of real estate-specific debt. When the cumulative debt bears too much risk, the lender will look to pool and sell some of its mortgages to, or buy the right to collect principal and mortgage payments from, other banks or investors. These mortgage-backed securities (MBS) are secured by different types of real estate, such as residential or commercial properties. Note that the terms of the mortgages do not change, so the property owner of record continues paying the same principal and interest.

The originators of MBS are generally the larger banks such as Morgan Stanley, Lehman Brothers and JP Morgan Chase. Before they pool their mortgages and issue the MBS, the originators must rate the debt – much like is done in the bond market. The rating gives the potential buyer an idea of the risk associated with the debt and ultimately impacts the cost of securities.

Let's focus on the commercial mortgage backed securities (CMBS) market and the third-party agencies hired to rate the debt. CMBS are secured by loans with commercial properties. Investors that buy CMBS purchase an undivided interest in a group of commercial mortgages. The agencies are hired by the issuer to provide an objective rating of the debt in exchange for a service fee. The rating is based on a report that is part financial analysis and part market analysis. Typically, the CMBS issuer hires more than one rating agency so the buyer can evaluate multiple ratings. Over the past ten years, the CMBS market has grown significantly, from $10 billion to $400 billion.

On the Job

The work atmosphere at a rating agency is team-oriented and focused on delivering an impartial analysis of the CMBS offering. Essentially, the agency does what the CMBS issuer originally did. It looks at the creditworthiness of the properties and debtors behind the mortgages.

Newcomers enter the field as analysts. Their responsibilities include data entry and financial modeling. Supervising the analyst is the director, whose main role is to collect and streamline all documents. The director is also a fact checker, often writes the final rating report and oversees the underwriting by the analyst. At this level the client interaction begins. Next in the hierarchy is the senior director who supervises all the work being done by the director and executes any requests from the client. Right above the senior director is the managing director, who usually has the banking relationships. This person's principal role is to get new work and smooth out any problems. The group managing director is at the top of the heap in the office. He's responsible for the business.

Although some rating agencies are international, the workload is often based on geography. Therefore, if you're on the East Coast, the deals you work on will most likely involve East Coast properties. Likewise, international deals are done by foreign offices.

Compensation

Agencies are paid a fee by CMBS issuers in return for their objective rating analysis. Each team member has the opportunity to make a bonus based on individual and group performance. As you ascend the hierarchy, the bonuses increase. An analyst makes roughly $40,000 per year plus a bonus. A director makes roughly $80,000-$120,000 per year plus a bonus. A senior director makes roughly $100,000-$150,000 per year plus a bonus. A managing director makes roughly $200,000 per year plus a bonus. The group managing director pulls in approximately $200,000-$250,000 per year plus a sizable bonus.

Getting Hired

You don't need to have a real estate license to work in this field. The main players in the rating business are Standard & Poors, Moody's and Fitch Ratings. The starting point is the analyst position; beyond this role it depends on the firm. "You don't have to have a real estate background to get in at the ground floor, but it does separate you from other candidates," says an insider at a leading rating agency. "We look for someone who is familiar with finance and, perhaps most importantly, we value interpersonal skills when filling an analyst position." This job has a reputation as a stepping stone to the investment side of the business.

In an interview, be ready to answer questions about the difference between equity and debt, the level of your Excel skills and what you like about real estate.

Questions to ask

- How does the team interact?

- What is the volume of transactions in the office?

- What is the level of turnover in the analyst position?

- What is the career path?

Questions to expect

- What is the difference between equity and debt?

- Why are you interested in real estate?

- How much finance have you been exposed to? (in school and your previous job)

- How strong are your Microsoft Excel skills?

- Are you a strong communicator?

For Further Reference

If you want to learn more about this area of the business, visit the Commercial Mortgage Securities Association web site at www.cmbs.org. There are also a few periodicals in this field such as *Commercial Mortgage Alert* (www.cmalert.com) and *Commercial Real Estate Direct* (find it on the Web at www.commercialrealestatedirect.com).

Visit Vault at **www.vault.com** for insider company profiles, expert advice, career message boards, expert resume reviews, the Vault Job Board and more.

VAULT CAREER LIBRARY

55

A Day in the Life of an Analyst at a CMBS Rating Agency

7:15 a.m.: Roll out of bed after only the second "snooze" break.

7:30 a.m.: Out the door and pick up *The Wall Street Journal* on the **corner.**

7:45 a.m.: Arrive at Terminal and board the Ferry to Pier 11 (Wall Street)

8:05 a.m.: Arrive at office. Settle in to cubicle: coffee, sports news, e-mails from the day before.

8:20 a.m.: Open new loan request package for $8 million on Garden Lakes Shopping Center in Portland, OR. Read it cover-to-cover (20 pages).

9:30 a.m.: Input financial particulars from package into Excel model for analysis.

10:00 a.m.: Make list of questions and concerns to ask broker/borrower that associate and vice president will want to have answered.

10:20 a.m.: Check for errors, save and print model.

10:30 a.m.: Call broker and ask questions. No answer, leave message.

10:35 a.m.: Visit associate's cubicle and get two new packages (loan requests) to review. Update her on progress and on current status of all my deals.

11:00 a.m.: Receive call from broker and get answers.

11:20 a.m.: Review new deal, $4 million loan request on Pacific Vistas Apartments in Newport Beach, CA. Input information into model.

12:20 p.m.: Get lunch with colleague at in-house cafeteria. Eat at desk.

1:00 p.m.: Stop by associate's desk to go over the Garden Lakes deal. He is not there, left note telling him that the deal is ready to go over.

1:10 p.m.: Finish Pacific Vistas model, check for errors, save and print.

1:15 p.m.: Call borrower's CFO (Chief Financial Officer) with questions about expense irregularities and source of "laundry income".

1:30 p.m.: Associate visits you and you go over both the Garden Lakes and Pacific Vistas deals. Open and tweak the computer models and change assumptions.

2:00 p.m.: With associate, stop by your supervising vice president's office to go over the two deals. We wait 5 minutes for him to finish a phone call with a borrower.

2:05 p.m.: Associate leads deal overview to VP, explaining that the company should lend no more than $7.5 million on Garden Lakes and could do the full $4 million on Pacific Vistas.

2:15 p.m.: VP makes changes to your model and assumptions. He calls broker on speakerphone and tells him of your intention to offer $7.65 million quote. The broker passes, telling you that three other lenders will give $8 million.

2:40 p.m.: VP calls the borrower's CFO on Pacific Vistas and tells him of your intention to issue a quote for $4 million with a low interest rate. The CFO verbally expresses interest.

3:00 p.m.: Draw up quote using a firm form sheet (WORD document).

3:30 p.m.: Take quote to associate for review, who edits and marks it up for change.

3:40 p.m.: Make changes to quote on Pacific Vistas.

Visit Vault at **www.vault.com** for insider company profiles, expert advice,
career message boards, expert resume reviews, the Vault Job Board and more.

VAULT CAREER LIBRARY   57

4:00 p.m.: Associate reviews and authorizes you to e-mail it out to the borrower.

4:05 p.m.: Issue the quote to the borrower via e-mail.

4:10 p.m.: Open new package, review information, and input model.

6:00 p.m.: The associate drops by, on her way out the door, to give you two new packages (a $10 million office building in Austin, TX and a $45 million portfolio of warehouses in New Jersey).

7:30 p.m.: Order dinner with other analysts. Eat in conference room with them.

9:00 p.m.: Shut down computer and order car service to take you home.

Real Estate Appraisal

CHAPTER 10

The Scoop

Real estate appraisal firms provide unbiased third-party estimates of a property's most probable sales price. Appraisals are typically performed for property sale, purchase refinancing. They're also used for tax appeals, bankruptcy, dispute resolution and monitoring the value of a real estate portfolio. Appraisers usually work for full-service real estate companies, banks or appraisal firms. Full-service real estate firms like CB Richard Ellis (www.cbre.com) and Cushman and Wakefield (www.cushwake.com) have valuation departments. Large banks, like Bank One and Wells Fargo, have appraisers on staff. In addition, there are specialty groups with larger appraisal firms like American Appraisal Associates. There are also a number of boutique appraisal firms in local markets, which are listed on the Appraisal Foundation's web site, which can be found at www.appraisalfoundation.org.

Once the buyer and seller of the property agree on the price, the lender requires an appraisal prior to closing to justify the price the buyer, its debtor, agreed to pay. Appraisals provide an objective third-party opinion on the value of the asset (or, in this case, real estate) underlying the proposed transaction to the creditors, who will finance the asset. The creditor usually agrees to lend the buyer the lesser of a certain percentage of either the appraised amount or the negotiated purchase price. If the appraisal of the property is well below the negotiated price, the creditor can back out of the deal or change the financing structure.

To perform a real estate appraisal in the U.S., you must be a licensed professional. Each state has its own real property appraiser regulatory program, which you must complete to become a licensed professional. Becoming a licensed professional in this field is much like becoming a real estate salesperson. You must complete several hours of education, pass a state exam and provide proof of relevant work experience.

You don't need a college education to become licensed. In Illinois, for example, there are three license levels: associate real estate appraiser, certified residential appraiser and certified general appraiser. The fee for each exam is $62. You can find information on getting a license, taking the exam or locations of the required classroom instruction on your state's appraisal licensing web site.

Visit Vault at **www.vault.com** for insider company profiles, expert advice, career message boards, expert resume reviews, the Vault Job Board and more.

VAULT CAREER LIBRARY   59

To obtain an associate license, you need to complete 75 classroom hours. For a certified residential license, you need 120 hours and 2,500 hours of practical work experience. For a certified general license, you need 180 hours and 3,000 hours of practical experience. At the end of classroom instruction, you have to pass a test before you're eligible to take the state license exam. An associate can't sign appraisal reports. Certified residential and general appraisers can sign off on appraisal reports, but only a general appraiser can work on residential and commercial assignments. Bear in mind that obtaining the more advanced licenses and designations can be expensive. For example, in Illinois, an associate can expect to pay $1,000 and up for other licenses and designations beyond the associate level. For more information about state-specific licensing requirements, you can contact the Appraisal Institute at (312) 335-4100 or visit their web site at www.appraisalinstitute.org. Remember that they don't issue licenses, just certifications and general information.

Many banks and real estate owners insist the appraisers they work with not only be licensed but designated professionals as well. Becoming a designated professional is harder than becoming a licensed professional; it's time consuming, and requires a college education.

There are several different certification organizations, each with their own criteria for certification. The Appraisal Institute (www.appraisalinstitute.org), one of the more respected licensing and certification organizations, issues the MAI and SRA designations. An MAI designation is for appraisers of residential, industrial and commercial properties, whereas SRA is for appraising residential real estate only.

To receive your MAI designation from the Appraisal Institute you must:

• Hold a college degree.

• Complete 380 classroom hours.

• Pass 11 instructional exams.

• Tally 6,000 hours of work experience.

• Participate in peer counseling.

• Write a demonstration report.

• Pass a comprehensive two-day exam.

The criteria for the SRA are:

• Hold a college degree.

- Complete 181 classroom hours.

- Pass 7 instructional exams.

- Tally 4,500 hours of work experience.

- Write a demonstration report.

Getting the MAI or SRA designation requires a lot of work but it may be worth it because you will be in higher demand, command higher fees and will be held in high regard by peers.

On the Job

This real estate career path is less cyclical than other real estate careers because appraisals are needed in both up and down markets. Even when the real estate industry is slow, many owners refinance – assuming interest rates are low – or audit their portfolio. Refinancing and auditing both require appraisals of the existing assets.

Appraisal is a trade-specific field. For some, the importance of information to the business may be a negative aspect of the career path. Clients expect detailed reports and writing the reports can be monotonous. Real estate appraisal is a very paper-intensive business.

The typical entry-level position in real estate appraisal involves a market research role. New hires are responsible for gathering market information for senior appraisers and help write reports that explain conclusions to the client. In this role, you spend a lot of time writing reports and doing research via the Internet and proprietary databases that house market information. A normal week is between 40-50 hours, but can go up to 60 hours.

As you become more experienced, you'll be expected to get an appraisal certification and will eventually be responsible for procuring new business. An appraiser interacts directly with the client, works with the market research associate to gather market comparables and local and general economic market conditions, does site inspections (which may translate into extensive travel), performs the valuation analysis and is responsible for the written report that presents the conclusions to the client.

As an appraiser, you'll learn about how the market values property as well as the concerns of the capital markets when investing in real estate. If you like real estate and finance, this is a great career to marry your two interests.

Visit Vault at **www.vault.com** for insider company profiles, expert advice, career message boards, expert resume reviews, the Vault Job Board and more.

VAULT CAREER LIBRARY   61

Typically, a lending institution would ask an appraiser to value a property or portfolio of properties for which they have or will issue debt. Once the research and the analysis necessary for the appraisal are complete, this information will be put into a written report and submitted to the client. The report often has a summary of the local or regional economy and may include demographic information. The following is an example of the DCF method in practice.

Real Estate Appraisal: A Case Study

You're hired to appraise a building using DCF that generates cash flow of $1,000,000 next year with five percent increase in cash flows for each of the next four years. The DCF will be for five years and the corresponding discount rate is 10 percent. Furthermore, you expect the reversionary value to be 5,000,000 and the cap rate to be nine. What is the value of the property? Plugging all the relevant information into the DCF formula and you get:

$$DCF = \frac{\$1,000,000}{(1.10)^1} + \frac{\$1,050,000}{(1.10)^2} + \frac{\$1,102,500}{(1.10)^3} + \frac{\$1,157,625}{(1.10)^4} + \frac{\$1,215,506}{(1.10)^5} + \frac{\{\$5,000,000 * 1/(1.10)^6\}}{.09}$$

Value = $38,875,103

Compensation

Appraisal is a fee-based service offered to lending institutions, who pay the firm a predetermined fee. In a property purchase, the buyer will reimburse the financing institution for the fee upon submitting its loan application. Don't expect to make a lot of money out the outset; new hires earn roughly $40,000 a year. Experienced appraisers earn $75,000 per year and up, depending on designation status and experience level. As you learn the trade, you'll become more valuable to your firm and will be paid more, so it's in your best interest to get certified as an appraiser.

Getting Hired

In addition to performing the requisite valuation analysis, an appraisal involves writing a succinct report for the client. That's why it's important for a candidate to demonstrate strong writing skills. A working knowledge of finance is also important because valuation formulas like the DCF are based on financial concepts. "I look for two things in new hires, writing skills and an understanding of finance," says Jules H. Marling IV, MAI and principal of Walden-Marling, Inc. an appraisal firm in Chicago. "In an interview, I expect the candidate to demonstrate that he or she has this skill set." Make sure to review the different methods of valuing real estate. If you're a good writer and have an understanding of finance, you should do well.

Expect questions about real estate valuation and what's happening with real estate values in your market (i.e., have an idea of local cap rates). Also be ready to explain basic finance principles like present value and discount rates. (See the real estate valuation sections in Chapter 3 and the Appendix, as well as *The Vault Guide to Finance Interviews* for more detail on valuation.)

"At some appraisal firms, there is a lack of advancement issue," Marling recommends. "Candidates should make sure to ask about the career path." If you want more information on finance concepts, visit www.investopedia.com – the site is free and a great resource.

Questions to ask

• What are the specific duties of an analyst at the company?

• Does the company sponsors employees when they seek designations?

• What types of clients and what types of appraisal projects does the firm handle?

Visit Vault at **www.vault.com** for insider company profiles, expert advice,
career message boards, expert resume reviews, the Vault Job Board and more.

VAULT CAREER LIBRARY

63

Use the Internet's
MOST TARGETED
job search tools.

Vault Job Board

Target your search by industry, function, and experience level, and find the job openings that you want.

VaultMatch Resume Database

Vault takes match-making to the next level: post your resume and customize your search by industry, function, experience and more. We'll match job listings with your interests and criteria and e-mail them directly to your inbox.

> VAULT
> the most trusted name in career information™

Property Management

CHAPTER 11

The Scoop

Real estate owners commonly employ professional property managers – either directly or through third-party management firms. Property managers are charged with the day-to-day management of real estate assets. They ensure that tenants are satisfied, the building is in good condition, rent is paid and that rents reflect market conditions. Property management provides a general introduction to real estate. As a property manager you'll learn how to efficiently operate a real estate asset in this capacity. Property managers deal with issues relating to leasing, construction, tenant relations and market analysis.

A good manager can save an owner a great deal of money by operating the asset efficiently and keeping the tenants happy. The property manager plays a crucial role in expense control; the owner relies on him to manage any and all operating expenses at the building. For instance, if there is construction work at the building, the property manager supervises the project, keeps close tabs on the progress and makes sure it doesn't go over budget. Property management also requires good interpersonal and analytical skills because tenants sometimes can be difficult and expect things to be resolved immediately. While leasing agents do much of the lease negotiations, property managers are involved in the process as well. A salesperson's license is therefore required for the position.

On the Job

The common entry-level point for this field is the position of assistant property manager (APM). APMs spend a good deal of the day fielding calls from tenants and owners. They're also charged with orchestrating any necessary repairs and dealing with vendors that provide services to the property. To top it off, they have the unpleasant task of making delinquency calls to tenants when they don't pay their rents. There is also administrative work such as assembling reports the property manager writes for owners as well as annual bid packages for any property work.

APMs report to a property manager (PM). PMs deal directly with the owner on all issues and are ultimately responsible for the day-to-day performance of the asset. The owner relies on them to maximize the real estate asset's net operating income. PMs report to a regional property manager (RPM). RPMs

Visit Vault at **www.vault.com** for insider company profiles, expert advice, career message boards, expert resume reviews, the Vault Job Board and more.

VAULT CAREER LIBRARY

65

are usually in charge of an entire region and interact with multiple owners. If an owner does have multiple properties, the RPM would be the point of contact. They're expected to bring in business and negotiate service contracts.

A typical day in property management might involve visiting one of your properties and talking on the phone with the owner, tenants and vendors. Property managers make sure accounts receivable (rent and other income brought in by the property) are in order.

Many owners expect timely reporting, so you'll also be gathering valuable market information that make up reports. This data may include rental rates in competitive buildings and lease rollover reports, which detail which leases are coming due at your property. PMs also write reports on rates of delinquency, rent patterns and reports on operations, which detail the physical condition of the property and the state of the budget.

Compensation

Careers in property management are generally salaried positions that include benefits. An assistant property manager should expect to make $30,000-$35,000 per year with a bonus based on individual performance and that of the asset(s). Property managers typically make a base salary of $70,000 per year and can expect an annual bonus. At properties where property managers handle lease renewals, owners sometimes pay commissions. This practice is not an industry standard but can be negotiated in the hiring package.

Getting Hired

"There are a few qualities that employers look for in property managers," says Heather Battaglia Higgins, assistant vice president at InterState Commercial in Chicago. "You must have strong people skills to handle both the tenants and the owners, be able to multitask, be willing to do administrative work and [you] must be comfortable with accounting."

In the interview, be ready to answer questions about your written and oral communication skills, as well as your organizational skills. You may be presented with a hypothetical situation involving an angry tenant and asked how you would resolve the issue.

Many employers require you to have a real estate license and a college education. In addition, some employers require that you have or obtain a property management designation. One of the more common designations is the certified property manager (CPM). To become a CPM you must have a high school diploma, be at least 18 years old, have a real estate license and complete classroom instruction, have at least five years of real estate experience. The CPM is specific to retail management. The cost of the application is $350 and the cost of classroom instruction is roughly $3,000. If you would like to work with office and industrial properties, you should obtain a real property administrator (RPA) designation. To get an RPA, you have to take seven classes plus a brief ethics course and demonstrate three years of property management experience. You can earn an RPA via self-study; it should take about two years to complete the classes and costs roughly $3,000.

Questions to ask

- How many properties are under management?

- What types of properties does the company manage? How many properties is an assistant property manager (or property manager) expected to work on?

- How many properties is a property manager expect to manage?

- *If the property manager is a a third-party manager:* How are the owners with whom the company works.

- *If the property manager is a a third-party manager:* Are they very demanding micromanagers or are they "hands off" managers?

Questions to expect

- Can you tell me about a project you completed that demonstrates strong organizational skills?

- Can you provide an example of a project or event that demonstrates strong people skills?

- Please describe how you would handle a client complaint.

- How strong is your understanding of basic accounting concepts?

Visit Vault at **www.vault.com** for insider company profiles, expert advice, career message boards, expert resume reviews, the Vault Job Board and more.

V/\ULT CAREER LIBRARY   67

For Further Reference

The RPA can be attained via self-study. If you elect to do the self-study route, it should take about two years to complete the required classes and costs roughly $3,000. You can learn more about becoming a CPM, RPA and general information on property management through the following sources:

- Institute of Real Estate (www.irem.org)
- Building Owners and Managers Institute (www.bomi-edu.org/index.html)
- Building Owners and Mangers Association (www.boma.org)

The larger full-service real estate firms, all have property management departments. Some of these include:

- CB Richard Ellis (www.cbre.com)
- Cushman & Wakefield (www.cushwake.com)
- Trammell Crow (www.trammelcrow.com)
- Jones Lang LaSalle (www.joneslanglasalle.com)

Real Estate Advisory

CHAPTER 12

The Scoop

Institutional investors, such as pension funds and insurance companies, are active in the real estate market. Wealthy individuals (sometimes referred to in the investment industry as high net worth individuals) also normally allocate a portion of their investment portfolio to property assets. As with the investments they make in stocks, bonds and other securities, institutional and individual investors often hire advisors to direct their real estate investments. Real estate advisors, or advisory firms as they are commonly known, act as a fiduciary agent. You'll sometimes hear people refer to this as the "agency" side of investing. Advisory firms help investors identify real estate assets that match their risk tolerance and targeted returns.

Advisory firms often raise equity for specific real estate investment objectives. For example, a firm may announce a fund that will focus on buying office properties in central business districts (CBDs). The advisory firms announce their intention to raise a fund and then solicit investors to contribute to the fund. Once the fund reaches its financial goal, it begins to identify properties for purchase and builds a portfolio. Advisory firms select investments by focusing on markets and property types likely to experience price appreciation in the future.

On the Job

Every advisory group operates differently, so the following description is a generalization. New hires start as associates and are expected to handle valuation analysis, as well as performance reporting to investors. The main task for associates is to run numbers and prepare reports for investors. The reports cover issues such as the state of the local market, taxes, valuation, local cap rates, buildings recently sold and the status of their cash flows. As an associate, you will be exposed to the inner workings of the group and receive on-the-job training. Associates in this field should understand that advancement in real estate advisory can be quite difficult. In fact, many advisory firms don't promote from the associate, hiring from outside the firm instead.

The next step up is portfolio associate (PA). In this role, you interact with the property manager on a regular basis to make sure the investment is in good working order. PAs still perform analysis but delegate much of this work to the associate. PAs might also make decisions on some smaller capital expenditures, such as repairs and upgrades to the building(s). In this position, you'll sit in on meetings to discuss acquisition assignments that involve your portfolio. PAs are asked to visit the buildings in their portfolio for site inspections. It's at this level that you begin to have client contact and are expected to understand the portfolio and anything related to the investments.

Above the PA is the portfolio manager (PM). The PM is responsible for the entire portfolio and everything related to the assets. All major decisions are made by the PM. The PM leads the charge on acquisitions and dispositions and is in constant communication with the client. He or she makes all major decisions related to the portfolio. Some advisory firms divide the portfolio manager duties among several people. For example, at some advisory firms, vice presidents tend to focus on one specific responsibility. They will either perform acquisitions, portfolio management or disposition of the assets.

At each advisory firm, individuals are assigned the task of raising money for the fund or finding clients. Some firms call these people market directors; others call them client relationship managers. In this role you are the representative of the advisory firm to the investment community and your sole function is to raise money. This is a sales-intensive role and extremely high profile in the real estate industry.

Compensation

Associates can expect a base salary competitive with the financial services industry, with a bonus based on department and individual performance. MBA graduates hired by advisory firms should expect to make between $85,000-$95,000 per year, plus a performance bonus. As with other MBA positions, a signing bonus is not uncommon. A non-MBA new hire should expect to be paid $40,000-$60,000, which includes any performance bonus. PAs should expect to make between $60,000-$90,000 including bonus, while PMs should expect to make over $100,000 a year plus bonus. Client relations managers and vice presidents normally make over $100,000, but pay may be more commission-oriented and hence more volatile.

Getting Hired

People who are comfortable with finance, especially valuation analysis, do well in this field. Strong interpersonal skills are also very important. Most firms look for people who already have worked in a finance and have some real estate experience, which is why they hire from MBA programs and investment banking. This is a very high profile and lucrative job, so it is arguably the most competitive career to land in real estate.

You must be comfortable with Microsoft Excel, as it's necessary for spreadsheet calculations and reporting. Many firms use a popular financial software package called ARGUS, which is specific to real estate and helps isolate project cash flows. Interviewers will likely ask if you're familiar with Excel and ARGUS and about your level of expertise with the software programs. In fact, one insider reports taking an Excel test to demonstrate that he knew how to model a real estate transaction.

The interviews are not entirely skills-based, of course. "We bring in people with at least two years experience and a financial background," says Albert Pura, a portfolio associate at RREEF. "In the interview, we focus on the individual to determine whether he or she will fit in our culture." "I was not asked one quantitative question during the interview process," adds Rich Monopoli, an MBA graduate from the Kellogg School of Management who took a job with Jones Lang LaSalle's Investment Management group. "I met with many people at the firm and got the sense that each one was determining if they would like working with me. That said, I was still ready to answer questions about valuation."

Questions to ask

• What are the day-to-day responsibilities?

• What is the career path and how common are internal promotions?

• Who are your clients?

• How much client interaction can one expect from this role?

Questions to expect

- Do you know ARGUS and if so, how much have you worked with the program?

- How is a real estate asset valued?

- What are the range of cap rates in this market for office buildings?

- If you were going to invest in a real estate, which type of asset would you buy and why?

For Further Reference

Some of the larger advisory firms are Jones Lang LaSalle (www.lasalle.com), RREEF (www.rreef.com) and Lend Lease (www.lendleaserei.com). These firms are larger, their names carry a lot of cache in the business, and they post jobs on their sites. You can also find out more about this field from the Pension Real Estate Association (www.prea.org).

You can download an ARGUS tutorial and trial version from its web site at www.argussoftware.com. If you're feeling particularly ambitious, you can take an ARGUS class. The site lists schools that offer training.

Real Estate Investment Banking

CHAPTER 13

The Scoop

Many investment banks on Wall Street and elsewhere have groups dedicated to real estate, which are good fits for someone with an interest in both real estate and investment banking. It shouldn't surprise you that these are very finance-oriented groups which look at real estate as one more asset class to make money for themselves and their partners. Products involve the repackaging of mortgages into residential mortgage-backed securities (MBS), collateralized mortgage obligations (CMOs) and commercial mortgage-backed securities (CMBS). Other popular areas include the REIT stock, bond and preferred stock origination business, lodging investment banking, principal investing in real estate and synthetic lease origination.

Some of the big players include Deutsche Bank (www.db.com), Goldman Sachs (www.gs.com), Morgan Stanley (www.morganstanley.com) and Lehman Brothers (www.lehman.com). These groups look to place money with operators (real estate developers and owners) all over the world who need capital for real estate projects. Operators, in turn, seek these groups out for funding. It's important to note that these groups look for high return deals. Of course, higher returns mean riskier deals. They base their decision on the expected return, or what is commonly referred to as the internal rate of return (IRR). You should know this term and be comfortable explaining it in an interview. Many people are intimidated by IRRs, but they're easy to understand. If you're discussing a potential investment, you will want to know the associated returns, which are expected but not guaranteed. That's what an IRR is: the expected return on the investment if everything goes according to plan.

Visit Vault at **www.vault.com** for insider company profiles, expert advice, career message boards, expert resume reviews, the Vault Job Board and more.

V/\ULT CAREER LIBRARY   73

IRR Example

Let's say that XYZ bank is going to invest $100 million in a real estate development today and in return expects to receive $10 million a year in cash flow for five years. Furthermore, the development will be sold at the end of the fifth year and XYZ's bank will receive $150 million in sale proceeds. The IRR is the expected return that is associated with this transaction. Remember, there are no guarantees related to the project only expectations – presumably, based on a good deal of analysis.

Note: There is a function in Excel that makes calculating the IRR very easy. Make sure to become familiar with this function.

On the Job

Entry-level employees, usually referred to as analysts, spend the bulk of their time doing acquisition/valuation work. They'll also do financial modeling for proposed deals. As part of the modeling, analysts account for the IRRs to the contributed debt and equity. Additionally, they help write deal memos that are presented to the investment committee, which ultimately makes the decision on whether or not the group will invest in the deal. The memo contains the pros and cons associated with the deal as well as market risk and fundamentals. In the course of preparing the memo, the analyst will have most likely visited the parties involved with the deal and inspected the physical asset. Since these groups invest money all over the world, there is a good deal of travel. At some companies, analysts have a lot of contact with the deal partners and will interact with the operators, attorneys and investors involved in the deal. They will seek any affecting the risk and return of the project.

The next level is the associate, whose main duty is to oversee the work of the analyst. He or she generally handles more of the contact with the deal partners and communicates any concerns or issues to the VP. Associates report to vice presidents (VPs), who have a supervisory role. Their main purpose is to bring in deals and make sure they run smoothly. Managing directors (MDs) are the top dogs in this hierarchy. They are even bigger dealmakers than the VPs and have the final call on all decisions. MDs are charged with business development.

Compensation

The pay is very good in this field. Analysts make anywhere from $60,000-$80,000 per year, with a supplemental bonus. The associate level is where the money becomes particularly enticing; associates can expect to make a base of $100,000 plus bonus. A VP's base salary is somewhere between $150,000 and $200,000 plus bonus. Managing directors can millions and have a major stake in the deals. All bonuses are contingent on group, project and individual performance. At some firms, anyone above the associate level has an equity position in the group.

Getting Hired

These jobs are very difficult to get because the real estate groups at I-banking firms tend to be small and you need a certain background. Candidates in this field have usually gone to a top undergraduate or business school and can demonstrate both an interest in finance and real estate. You don't need a real estate license for a career in real estate investment banking, but many people belong to industry organizations like the Urban Land Institute (www.uli.org).

If you get an interview, be conversant in the condition of the world economy and the general health of the real estate market. Be ready to answer questions about IRRs, discount rates, PVs and why you have an interest in the industry

Questions to ask

• How may deals have you completed over the past few years?

• What is the typical size (money wise) of the deal?

• Does the company focus in one sector of real estate?

• In this role how will someone interact with the rest group?

• What is the natural progression from this role? (Specifically, will you be expected to have your MBA to take the leap from associate to vice president?)

Questions to expect

• Are you comfortable calculating Internal Rates of Returns (IRRs)?

• What type of financial modeling have you done in the past?

• What are your thoughts on the current state of the domestic economy?

Visit Vault at **www.vault.com** for insider company profiles, expert advice, career message boards, expert resume reviews, the Vault Job Board and more.

VAULT CAREER LIBRARY

75

• If you were investing in real estate which markets (geographically) would you place your money and why?

• How much do you know about our group and its performance?

Development

CHAPTER 14

The Scoop

If you enjoy taking risks, look no further than development. Development involves managing labor, establishing time estimates, managing money and monitoring construction crews. Good developers are results-oriented, creative and know how to get work done on time. You can break into the field by working for a smaller developer or you can strike out on your own, starting with some smaller transactions.

In development, you take a concept and physically construct or alter a property that will last for years. In this field, you work with the local and sometimes federal government to bring your project to life. You also aggressively pursue necessary funding from both the debt and equity markets to make the project a reality. Because of changes in population, technology and consumer taste, there's always a need for development.

Even the largest developers have lean organizations, so getting a job is tough. Some developers specialize as design-build firms that help design and then build real estate for a fee, while other developers are full-service firms that not only design and build the property, but manage and lease it after the building is completed. Most real estate professionals agree that development is the riskiest, most rewarding part of the industry. Many developers are extremely charismatic and appear regularly in the society pages. It seems that every major city has its own Donald Trump – someone behind the high-profile real estate projects and deals.

One of the best things about real estate is the lifestyle and development is no exception. "This is definitely a work hard, play hard career," said one real estate developer. Since much of the job is focused on cultivating personal relationships, co-workers are typically gregarious folk who love to have a good time. "I worked in banking before I made the jump to development," another professional in development confides. "I saw how much fun and money my real estate clients were having and decided to switch careers. Granted there is a learning curve and you initially suffer pay-wise, but I don't know any industry that allows you to make the kind of money you can make in real estate, while not putting in a ridiculous amount of hours."

Visit Vault at **www.vault.com** for insider company profiles, expert advice, career message boards, expert resume reviews, the Vault Job Board and more.

VAULT CAREER LIBRARY 77

On the Job

The developer is the person or the company responsible for creating the concept of a property and bringing it to reality. One thing must be stressed: Every development firm is different, more so than in any other part of the real estate industry. Titles and pay scales vary widely from firm to firm.

New hires normally start as analysts, creating and revising spreadsheets that examine returns for the developer. Part of the spreadsheet analysis is keeping track of debt payments and the returns to equity partners. In this role, you'll be expected to become a Microsoft Excel expert since your principal duty will be to run financial spreadsheets. Any time there is a change to the project, the analyst reruns the spreadsheets to determine how it impacts the developer's and investors' returns. Since most development firms are lean, analysts can expect to perform other duties such as market research, studying comparable project research, leasing activity in your market and demographic studies.

Associates, sometimes called project managers, work above analysts and are assigned to a specific project. The developer may have 10 buildings under construction, but the associate will usually be responsible for only one of them. Associates still perform financial analysis, but have additional duties such as contact with the real estate community and the development partners – architect, contractor, investors and attorneys. Your main task is to ensure that the building is constructed on time. The management team will rely on you for updates and recommendations. You write a number of memos and begin to get invited to presentations to management.

Associates report to vice presidents (VPs), which at some companies are called managing directors (MDs). They're responsible for multiple assignments and make the final decisions with respect to the development project or portfolio. VPs delegate a lot of work to associates but are ultimately responsible for a development's success. They're directly involved with leasing or sale negotiations and report to management or the developer. In this role, there's a lot of responsibility and a ton of pressure.

At many development firms, you will have the opportunity to eventually become a principal. As such you'll be expected to contribute equity to a development. Principals are asked to help raise money and are also expected to provide concepts for future developments. This is as good as it gets in the industry: you can make millions.

Developers start marketing their projects before they break ground and will often have their own team of leasing agents to market the property to the real estate community and show it to prospects. Leasing agents who work for developers essentially have the same responsibilities as regular agents, but are under much more pressure when leasing a new development. Junior agents are assigned to a project and work with the leasing team to market the property and conduct property tours. It is worth pointing out, however, that some leasing agents at development firms eventually become principals.

Compensation

Analysts can make between $40,000-$50,000 per year. There is bonus potential, but at this level don't expect much. Associates at the larger firms make roughly $80,000-$90,000 per year. At this level, you have the potential to make a bonus of 10 to 20 percent of your salary. At the vice president's level, the money becomes very good, with a base salary of anywhere from $150,000 on up. On top of this, you can earn a bonus as high as your salary. Principals can make millions; it all depends on how the project(s) perform.

Getting Hired

If you know you want to pursue a role in development, be extra-aggressive; even the largest developers are lean and don't add staff often. For those at business schools, be ready to perform an independent job search. Chances are your career placement office doesn't bring a lot of firms to campus or is simply not familiar with this field.

Developers will expect you to tell them why you're interested in this particular field. Be prepared to describe how to value a property and what makes it valuable. Be able to discuss the local real estate markets, including vacancy rates, rental rates and current development projects. Brace yourself for questions about time management, organizational and interpersonal skills. One insider says many developers like people with marketing skills, which makes sense – effectively marketing yourself and the project you're working on will ensure your success.

Questions to ask

• As the field is very cyclical and development slows when the economy is weak, what does the staff do when the company is between projects?

• Can you walk me through some recent projects from start to finish?

- Are most projects the firm works on rehabilitation projects or new developments?

- Does the company focus on one real estate sector?

- What is the firm's organizational structure like? Which team members focus on identifying opportunities; which concentrate on raising money?

- How does the firm raise funds for projects? Is the firm using banks, insurance companies, wealthy individuals or other money sources?

- What are your targeted returns or IRRs?

Questions to ask

- What is your understanding of the development process?

- What recent well-known development do you think highly of and why?

- Can you describe some local high profile developments?

- What is your understanding of finance and how it plays a role in development?

For Further Reference

If you want to learn more about development, read *Urban Land* (www.uli.org), *Realtor* (www.nar.org), *Journal of Real Estate Portfolio Management* (www.aresnet.org) and *National Real Estate Investor* (www.nerionline.com). You can't buy these at your local newsstand, but you can visit their web sites and learn more about developments across the country. Most people cin this field choose to join the Urban Land Institute (www.uli.org).

There are companies out there hiring MBAs, but you have dig to find them. Two well-known companies are Hines (www.hines.com) and Trammell Crow (www.trammellcrow.com). Both have good web sites and list available jobs.

Conclusion

After reading this guide you should have come to the following conclusions:
1.) The real estate industry is a tight-knit community. 2.) When looking for
a job, it pays to be aggressive. 3) There are many different roles available to
the ambitious job seeker.

To get the job you want, use resources such as your alma mater's alumni
network, real estate related web sites such as those listed in the Appendix and
network within the industry as much as possible. Remember, most real estate
jobs are filled by word of mouth, so build your own network within the real
estate community. Once you get the interview, be ready to demonstrate your
passion for the industry.

Good luck!

Visit Vault at **www.vault.com** for insider company profiles, expert advice,
career message boards, expert resume reviews, the Vault Job Board and more.

VAULT CAREER LIBRARY

81

Use the Internet's
MOST TARGETED
job search tools.

Vault Job Board

Target your search by industry, function, and experience level, and find the job openings that you want.

VaultMatch Resume Database

Vault takes match-making to the next level: post your resume and customize your search by industry, function, experience and more. We'll match job listings with your interests and criteria and e-mail them directly to your inbox.

VAULT
> the most trusted name in career information™

APPENDIX

Industry Buzzwords

Abatement: A reduction or concession that the landlord offers the tenant. Generally referred to in terms of rent or other would-be escalations.

Above building standard: Refers to items above and beyond what the landlord typically will include in a standard office build out for tenants.

Absorbed space: The net change, either positive or negative, of the amount of real estate available during a period in a given area (usually stated in square feet).

Absorption rate: The percentage of space in a market that is either leased or given back to the real estate market in a stated period. Used as a measurement of supply and demand.

> **Positive absorption:** available space that has been leased or taken off the market.
>
> **Negative absorption:** space that is added to the market (i.e. new construction or space that was previously leased and has since become vacant).

Addendum: A document that includes any additions or changes to items in the original lease. Items in an addendum take precedence to items being replaced in the lease.

Add-On Factor: also known as a loss factor, common area factor or core factor. Comprised of the building areas that are common or used by all tenants. The common areas include, but are not limited to: lobbies, restrooms, corridors, storage rooms, electrical rooms and janitorial closets.

Adjustable-rate mortgage (ARM): A mortgage where the interest can fluctuate during the loan. The interest will change at different intervals pursuant to loan terms. These are typically short term and payments are less than most fixed loans. They're sometimes preferred when homebuyers do not anticipate staying in the home for a long time or if the homebuyer believes that interest rates will drop.

Ad valorem: Property taxes based on the government's valuation of the property.

Amenities: Features that enhance the value of the property. Includes health clubs, sundry stores, restaurants, daycare and parking.

Visit Vault at **www.vault.com** for insider company profiles, expert advice, career message boards, expert resume reviews, the Vault Job Board and more.

VAULT CAREER LIBRARY   85

Amendment: An alteration or change to the original lease. These will have been accepted by all parties and recorded in a separate document.

Americans with Disabilities Act (ADA): Specific federal property requirements that need to be made available for the handicap.

Amortization: Spreading loan payments of principal and interest over a certain time period.

Annual operating expense increase/overages: Applicable to Full Service or Gross Leases. The operating expenses that reflect the tenant's proportionate share of the building's total operating expense costs greater than the original estimate provided by the Landlord. Costs are stated in square feet.

> **Base year:** When the Landlord quotes operating expenses on a specific base year, the tenant is responsible for the difference between the operating expenses in the base year stated in the lease and the current operating expenses. For example assume the base year is 2000 and the operating expenses in that year are $12.00 per square foot. Further assume that in 2002 operating expenses are $15.00 per square foot. The tenant would pay $3.00 per square foot.

> **Expense stop:** For example, the Landlord may state the building's expense stop as $10.00 per square foot. This means that the Landlord pays the first $10.00 per square foot of building operating expenses. If the building operates at greater than the estimated $10.00, the tenant pays the difference.

APR (Annual Percentage Rate): Stated as a percentage of the loan. Includes all fees related to the loan.

Annual rental rate: The cost, usually calculated in square feet, to lease space in a building. If the rent is stated in square feet you multiply the rent by the amount of leased square feet to arrive at your annual rent obligation. For example if a tenant is leasing 10,000 square feet at $30 per square foot that equals annual rent of $300,000 (note, that certain markets quote rent per square feet on an annual basis whereas others do so on a monthly basis. Watch your conversions!)

Appraisal: An opinion of value given on a property. Should be based on information that is certified by a licensed appraiser.

Appreciation: Occurs when the property's value increases.

Assessment: An estimation of a property's value. Generally used to calculate the tax obligation per property.

Assignment of lease: The transfer of all responsibilities and liabilities of the lease from one party to another.

Base rent: The initial rental rate for leasing property. Note, the base rent may be subject to annual increases. Any escalations are calculated off the base rent.

Base year: A stated year from which operating costs or other escalations are then projected. When the landlord quotes on a specific base year, the tenant is responsible for the difference between the operating expenses in the base year stated in the lease and the current operating expenses. For example, assume the base year is 2000 and the operating expenses in that year are $12.00. Then assume that in 2002 operating expenses are $15.00. The tenant would pay $3.00 per square foot. (See annual operating expense increase/overages.)

B.O.M.A.: The Building Owners and Manager's Association. An international organization that provides recommended guidelines to be used in negotiations between commercial landlords and tenants. B.O.M.A.'s measurement calculations are widely accepted to calculated leased space.

Broker: An intermediary that acts on behalf of a landlord, tenant, owner or purchaser. A broker that acts on behalf of the tenant is referred to as a "Tenant Representative", whereas a broker that acts on behalf of the landlord is called a "Building or Landlord Representative." A broker is common to all facets of real estate.

Build-out: Refers to the construction of the tenant's proposed space, to make it ready for occupancy, or to comply with tenant's construction needs according to the terms and conditions of the lease. Also referred to as TIs (Tenant Improvements)

Build to suit: Constructing a premises or facility per a tenant's specifications.

Capitalization rate: Also referred to as a "cap rate." Derived from taking the property's expected net income and dividing it by the sales price. The ratio is a market measuring stick that is commonly referenced. When cap rates are low, properties are selling at a premium; when cap rates are high, property prices drop.

Cash flow: The cash receipts generated from a building, net of operating expenses, taxes, insurance and other transactions costs such as: tenant improvements and commissions.

Certificate of occupancy (C.O.): A document issued by the local governmental authorities, stating that the building or office space is in the proper condition to be occupied.

Close of escrow: The point where seller gets paid and the buyer takes possession of the property.

Closing costs: Fees that the buyer and seller incur as a result of the property transaction. The down payment is not included but all other costs such as legal fees, insurance and property taxes are part of this calculation.

Commission: A market fee generally paid to the broker for representing a party in either a property sale or lease negotiation.

Common area maintenance fees: commonly referred to as "CAM." In retail it's a fee charged to tenants to maintain the outward and overall appearance of the property. In the office building industry it's generally interchangeable with overage of operating expenses.

Comparables: Similar properties used as a comparison to determine a fair market value.

C.P.I. (Consumer Price Index): An index that is used to track inflation. Many escalations in leases are tied to this index. In most leases, this is used as the basis for adjusting annual rent increases.

Covenant: A promise or assurance given by one party to another. Another definition is a legal restriction of property.

Debt: Money that is borrowed. The debtor is contractually bound to repay the lender.

Debt service: Payments made toward a loan.

Deed: A written instrument by which title to property is conveyed.

Depreciation: A decrease in a property's value.

Down payment: The amount of money that the purchaser is contributing toward the property purchase. Many times a lender will require a minimum down payment for a loan. For example, if a house costs $500,000 and the bank to which you are applying for a loan requires a minimum 20 percent down payment, you are expected to contribute $100,000.

Easement: A right to access another property owner's land for a specific purpose.

Eminent domain: A right reserved by the government to seize property by condemnation while proving consideration for the owner.

Encumbrance: A claim or lien filed against a property.

Equity: An individual or institution's ownership position in a property.

Expense stop: An established dollar amount towards operating expenses of the building that the landlord is willing to pay. The tenant will be required to pay his proportionate share of any costs above (or over) this predetermined amount. For example, a landlord may state the building's expense stop as $10.00. This means that the landlord pays the first $10.00 of building operating expenses. If the building operates at a cost greater than the estimated $10.00, the tenant pays the difference.

Fair market value: The price that a property would likely yield in the current market.

Fixed-rate mortgage: The interest rate is the same for the life of the loan. Typically involves a long-term loan such as a 30-year fixed rate mortgage. People prefer this loan when they expect to stay in the home for a long time. The payments remain the same for the life of the loan.

Full service lease: A commercial lease that is also known as a "Gross Lease." The tenant makes one rent payment to landlord to cover both tenant's rent and operating expenses obligation.

General contractor: An individual or company that coordinates and supervises all construction.

Gross lease: See full service lease.

Gross Square Footage: The property's total square footage without making any allowances.

HVAC: The heating, air-conditioning and other ventilation systems within property.

Landlord: The owner or operator of the property.

Lease: Legal document that outlines the terms and condition under which a landlord agrees to lease space to a tenant and vice versa.

Leasee: Individual or company that leases space at a property.

Leasing agent: Individual that leases space at the property.

Lessor: Property owner that leases space to a leasee.

Visit Vault at **www.vault.com** for insider company profiles, expert advice, career message boards, expert resume reviews, the Vault Job Board and more.

VAULT CAREER LIBRARY   **89**

Lien: Claim against property.

Load factor or loss factor: Also known as common area factor. Represents the percentage difference between the rentable and usable square footage in the building.

Loan-to-value (LTV) ratio: The percentage of the home's value that is borrowed. This LTV ratio is commonly referred to in banking because many lenders have LTV limit policies. If a property that was worth $1,000,000 had a loan of $800,000, its LTV would be 80 percent.

Mixed use building: A structure that has more than one particular use.

Modified gross lease: Similar to a gross lease in that all costs, rent for premises as well as tenant's proportionate share of building's operating expenses are included, except that in the event the operating expenses exceed the landlord's estimate, the tenant pays the overage.

Mortgage: Legal instrument where real property is security for the payment of a loan. In the event that the borrower defaults its loan obligations, the lender can "foreclose" on the property.

Negative absorption: Space that is added to the market (i.e. new construction or space that was previously leased and has since become vacant).

Net lease: Opposite of the full service or gross lease. In this lease structure, tenant is responsible for the direct payment of its share of operating expenses.

Net operating income: Gross income produced at the building minus operating expenses.

Operating expenses: The landlord's cost to operate the property. Typical expenses include real estate taxes, utilities, insurance, maintenance and repairs, janitorial, property management, security and labor associated with the building.

Operating expense pass-throughs: Specific operating expenses that are passed on to the tenant in order to operate the building. Typically, the tenant pays its proportionate share of operating expenses, which is based on the percentage of the building that the tenant occupies.

Origination fee: Also referred to as "points." The fee that the lender will charge for the mortgage. The expression "point" refers to a percentage point of the loan. Therefore if you were charged two points by the bank to process your loan of $100,000 you would owe $2,000 in fees.

Percentage lease: When rent is based on a percentage of a tenant's sales. (Common to retail leases.)

Positive absorption: Available space that has been leased or taken off the real estate market.

Principal: The amount of the loan that does not include any interest.

Property: Two classifications: real and personal. Real property is land and any improvements on that land. Everything else is considered personal property. (This book is concerned only with real property.)

Pro-rata share: Percentage of the building's total rentable square feet that is occupied by the tenant.

Punch list: List of items that the tenant or buyer expects the landlord or seller to repair, before they take possession of the property.

Rent: What the tenant pays the landlord in return for the right to occupy the premises.

Rentable square footage: The amount of square feet, including the common area factor of the building. This typically is the square footage the tenant will pay rent on.

Rental rate: Rate at which the tenant leases the premises from the landlord.

Security deposit: Amount of money required by the landlord from the tenant, that the landlord can access in the event that the tenant defaults or damages the premises.

Space plan: Architectural drawing of the tenant's desired construction of its leased premises.

Sublease: During the lease term when the tenant leases the premises to a third party – that is from then on referred to as the subtenant. Unless it has been pre-negotiated, tenant must seek the approval from landlord.

Tenant: Individual or institution that leases space from the Landlord.

Tenant improvements: Enhancements that are done by the tenant to its leased premises.

Tenant improvement allowance: The amount, or allowance, that the landlord will provide to the tenant for the construction or build out of its leased premises. The amount is usually stated in terms of square feet.

Title: Legal documentation of ownership.

Triple net rent: Rent structure where the tenant pays all expenses in addition to its rent.

Usable square footage: The actual square footage in a tenant's premises. Calculated by taking the rentable square feet and subtracting the load factor.

Vacancy factor: The amount of space not occupied in a particular building or, if referring to the entire market, the amount of total vacant space in the real estate market.

Warranty: Assurances given from the seller to the buyer or building owner to the tenant.

Zoning: Governmental ordinances that specify the use or uses that are permitted in an area or on a property.

Concept Overview: Net Operating Income

If you plan on entering the investment side of real estate, you should become familiar with net operating income (NOI). Simply stated, NOI is the income generated by a property minus the expenses at the building. It's used in calculating the value of the property.

The example below demonstrates how you arrive at NOI. There's a brief explanation of each line item.

Income

   Potential Gross Rent

   + Parking Income (if applicable)

   = Potential Gross Income

   - Vacancy Loss

   = Effective Gross Income

Expenses

   Operating Expenses

   + Real estate taxes

   + Cash reserve

   = Total Expenses

Effective Gross Income – Total Expenses = Net Operating Income

The potential gross income is the total available rentable square feet in the building multiplied by the annual rent per square foot. If the building has parking, parking revenue should be added to arrive at potential gross income. Thus far the assumption was that the entire building was leased. In reality, that's not always the case. We must account for the vacant portion of the building for which we are not collecting rent, so we subtract this vacancy loss from the potential gross income to arrive at the effective gross income.

Next we have to consider our expenses to run the building. There are the operating expenses such as utilities and cleaning costs to consider as well as real estate taxes that we need to pay. Finally, we allot a budget or cash reserve to account for other expenses that may come up. Collectively, these are our total expenses. The last step is to subtract the total expenses from the effective gross income, which equals NOI.

Business Schools with Real Estate Programs

CHAPTER 8

MIT Sloan School of Management www.mitsloan.mit.edu

Wharton www.wharton.upenn.edu/mba

Haas School of Business www.haas.berkeley.edu/mba

University of Wisconsin www.bus.wisc.edu/graduateprograms/fulltime

The Kellogg School of Management www.kellogg.northwestern.edu

Fisher College of Business – The Ohio State University www.cob.ohio-state.edu

Visit Vault at **www.vault.com** for insider company profiles, expert advice, career message boards, expert resume reviews, the Vault Job Board and more.

VAULT CAREER LIBRARY   95

Web Resources

Real Estate Organizations

Appraisal Foundation www.appraisalfoundation.org

Appraisal Institute www.appraisalinstitute.org

Building Owners and Managers Association International (BOMA) www.boma.org

Certified Commercial Investment Member www.ccim.com

Counselors of Real Estate www.cre.org

International Council of Shopping Centers (ICSC) www.icsc.org

Mortgage Bankers Association of America www.mbaa.org

NACREIF www.nacreif.com

NAOIP www.naiop.org

NAR www.realtor.com

National Association of Real Estate Investment Managers www.nareim.org

National Association of Real Estate Investment Trusts (NAREIT) www.nareit.com

National Multi Housing Council www.nmhc.org

Pension Real Estate Association www.prea.org

Society of Industrial and Office Realtors www.sior.com

The Institute of Real Estate Management www.irem.org

ULI www.uli.org

Urban Land Institute www.uli.org

Periodicals

Globe Street www.globest.com

Commercial Property News www.cpnonline.com

Journal of Property Investment and Finance

Real Estate Alert www.realert.com

Realty Stock Review www.reri.org

Midwest Real Estate News www.mwreonline.com

National Real Estate Investor www.nreionline.com

Multifamily Executive www.multifamilyexecutive.com

General Site for Periodicals

Global Software Solutions
www.globalsoftwaresolutions.net/realestate/publications.htm

General Information

Real Estate ABCs www.realestateabc.com

Real Estate Employers

CHAPTER 2

Residential Real Estate Companies

RE/MAX

Headquarters:
8390 E. Crescent Parkway, Suite 500/600
Greenwood Village, CO 80111-2800
P.O. Box 3907
Englewood, CO 80155-3907
Phone: (303) 770-5571
www.remax.com

One of the largest residential real estate brokers with 78,000 employees. In exchange for paying a management fee and a share of the monthly office overhead, RE/MAX agents receive commissions and receive the many benefits of RE/MAX programs and services. These offices operate as franchises. The web site offers information on becoming a sales associate.

Coldwell Banker Real Estate Corporation

Headquarters:
1 Campus Drive
Parsippany, NJ 07054
Phone: (973) 428-9700
www.coldwellbanker.com

Coldwell Banker's parent company is Cendant Corporation, which also owns Century 21. Coldwell Banker has more than 3,000 independently owned and operated residential and commercial real estate offices with over 75,000 sales associates internationally and is known primarily for representing buyers and sellers in the residential real estate market. You can search the company's web site to find the office nearest you or send an e-mail through a link on the site to the corporate office with any career questions.

Century 21 Real Estate Corporation

Headquarters:
1 Campus Drive
Parsippany, New Jersey 07054
Phone: (877) 221-2765
www.century21.com

Also owned by Cendant Corporation, Century 21 Real Estate Corporation is the franchisor of the world's largest residential real estate sales organization, with more than 6,600 independently owned and operated franchised broker offices in over 30 countries and territories worldwide. Their agents represent both buyers and sellers of residential real estate. The firm is known for good training programs.

Full Service Commercial (property management, leasing, investment, brokerage)

Cushman and Wakefield

Headquarters:
51 West 52nd Street
New York, NY 10019-6178
Phone: (212) 841-7500
www.cushwake.com

A leading provider of commercial real estate services. Clients include landlords, tenants and investors. Offers advisory services, valuation advice, strategic planning, research, portfolio analysis and site selection. Candidates can view job openings by city on the corporate web site. The appropriate contacts are also listed on the site.

ICB Richard Ellis

Headquarters:
355 South Grand Avenue
Suite 200
Los Angeles, CA 90071
Phone: (213) 613-3333
www.cbre.com

CB Richard Ellis is a global provider of commercial real estate services. It has 10,000 employees in more than 250 offices across 47 countries. CB, as it is commonly known, offers brokerage assistance, corporate services, research, consulting, project management, valuation and advisory. CB Richard Ellis acquired Insignia/ESG in 2003. Candidates can send their resumes to opps@cbre.com.

Jones Lang LaSalle

Headquarters:
200 East Randolph Drive
Chicago, IL 60601
Phone: (312) 782-5800
www.joneslanglasalle.com

Jones Lang LaSalle is a leading international provider of comprehensive real estate and investment management services. The company stresses a team environment and serves clients locally, regionally and internationally from offices in over 100 markets on five continents. The 7,200 Jones Lang LaSalle professionals offer integrated investment, transaction, and management services. In recent years, the firm has been known to recruit MBAs from Kellogg and the University of Chicago and career switchers. Also, while most of their competitors pay commissions only, Jones Lang LaSalle pays base salaries. Candidates can view jobs and submit resumes online at the corporate web site.

Visit Vault at **www.vault.com** for insider company profiles, expert advice, career message boards, expert resume reviews, the Vault Job Board and more.

VAULT CAREER LIBRARY   **101**

Development

Catellus

Headquarters:
201 Mission Street, 2nd Floor
San Francisco, CA 94105
Phone: (415) 974-4500
www.catellus.com

Catellus Development Corporation is one of the nation's premier diversified
real estate development companies. The company specializes in developing,
managing and investing in a broad range of product types including
industrial, office, residential, retail and major urban development projects. It
owns a portfolio of rental properties totaling 37 million square feet and one
of the largest supplies of developable land in the western United States.

Hines

Headquarters:
Williams Tower
2800 Post Oak Boulevard
Houston, TX 77056
Phone: (713) 621-8000
HR contact: Tracy Smith
E-mail: tracy_smith@hines.com
www.hines.com

An international developer that has planned and executed more than 650
projects including skyscrapers, corporate headquarters, mixed-use centers,
industrial parks, and master-planned resort and residential communities.
Currently, Hines has over 78 million square feet under management and
controls assets valued in excess of $13 billion. The firm has offices
throughout the U.S. and in 11 other countries including: the United Kingdom,
France, Spain, Mexico, Poland, Russia, Germany, Brazil, Italy, Argentina and
China. It has been known to recruit people with engineering backgrounds
amd court MBAs.

KB Homes

Headquarters:
10990 Wilshire Boulevard
7th Floor
Los Angeles, California 90024
Phone: (310) 231-4000
www.kbhome.com

KB Home is one of America's largest homebuilders with domestic operating divisions in Arizona, California, Colorado, Florida, Nevada, New Mexico and Texas. Kaufman & Broad S.A., the Company's majority-owned subsidiary, is one of the largest homebuilders in France. In fiscal 2002, the company delivered 25,565 homes in the United States and France. It also operates KB Home Mortgage Company, a full-service mortgage company for the convenience of its buyers. All openings can be viewed on the company web site and entries can be submitted online.

Tishman Speyer Properties

Headquarters:
520 Madison Avenue
New York, New York 10022
Phone: (212) 715-0300
www.tishmanspeyer.com

Tishman Speyer Properties is a leading international owner/operator and developer of office buildings with nine domestic offices as well as some in Europe and Latin America. All job openings are listed on the company web site and entries can be submitted online.

Trammell Crow

Headquarters:
2001 Ross Avenue
Suite 3400
Dallas, Texas 75201
Phone: (214) 863-3000
www.trammellcrow.com

Trammell Crow emphasizes three core services of building management, brokerage, and development and project management. The firm focuses on two customers: users of commercial real estate and facilities, and investors in commercial real estate. Applicants should have expertise in office, industrial, and retail properties.

REITs

Office-focused

Boston Properties, Inc.

Headquarters:
111 Huntington Avenue
Boston, MA 02199-7602
Phone: (617) 236-330
www.bostonproperties.com

Boston Properties, Inc. is a self-administered and self-managed REIT that develops, redevelops, acquires, manages, operates and owns a diverse portfolio of Class A office, industrial and hotel properties. The company is one of the largest owners, acquirers and developers of Class A office properties in the U.S., concentrated in four core markets – Boston; Washington, DC; midtown Manhattan; and San Francisco. Founded in 1970, its primary focus is office space. However, its property portfolio also includes hotels and industrial buildings. Boston Properties has five full-service regional offices located in the aforementioned areas and Princeton, New Jersey.

Equity Office

Headquarters:
Two North Riverside Plaza
Chicago, IL 60606
Phone: (312)-466-3300
www.equityoffice.com

The nation's largest office building owner and property manager, as well as the largest REIT in the United States. Widely considered the premier REIT and an innovator in the industry. Run by Sam Zell, one of the most highly regarded real estate minds in the world. Owns buildings in virtually every major city and has related real estate companies who focus on other facets of real estate. All openings can be viewed on the company web site and applications can be submitted online.

Retail-focused

General Growth Properties

Headquarters:
110 North Wacker Drive
Chicago, IL 60606
Phone: (312) 960-5000
www.generalgrowth.com

General Growth Properties, Inc. is a real estate investment trust (REIT) engaged in the ownership, operation, management, leasing, acquisition, development, expansion and financing of regional mall shopping centers in the United States. As of December 31, 2001, General Growth either directly or through the operating partnership and subsidiaries owned 100% of 54 regional mall shopping centers and 50% of each of two regional mall shopping centers. All openings can be viewed on the company web site and applications can be submitted online.

Simon Property Group, Inc.

Headquarters:
115 West Washington Street
Indianapolis, Indiana 46204
Phone: (317) 636-1600
www.shopsimon.com

Simon Property Group, Inc., is a REIT that owns and manages income-producing properties, primarily regional malls and community shopping centers. Through its subsidiary partnerships, it currently owns or has an interest in 246 properties containing an aggregate of 184 million square feet of gross leasable area in 36 states, as well as eight assets in Europe and Canada. It is the largest publicly traded retail real estate company in North America with a total market capitalization of approximately $21.3 billion as of December 31, 2002. All openings can be viewed on the company web site and applications can be submitted online.

Visit Vault at **www.vault.com** for insider company profiles, expert advice,
career message boards, expert resume reviews, the Vault Job Board and more.

VAULT CAREER LIBRARY   105

Industrial

AMB Property Corp.

Headquarters:
Pier 1 Bay 1
San Francisco, CA 94111
Phone: (415) 394-9000
www.amb.com

AMB Property Corporation is a REIT engaged in the acquisition, ownership, operation, management, renovation, expansion and development of primarily industrial properties nationwide. Through its subsidiary, AMB Capital Partners, LLC, AMB also manages industrial buildings and retail centers, totaling approximately 2.7 million rentable square feet on behalf of various clients. In addition, the company has invested in 40 industrial buildings, totaling approximately 4.9 million rentable square feet through unconsolidated joint ventures. All openings can be viewed on the company web site and applications can be submitted online.

ProLogis Trust

Headquarters:
14100 East 35th Place
Aurora, CO 80011
Phone: (303)375-9292
www.prologis.com

ProLogis Trust operates a global network of industrial distribution facilities. ProLogis' business is organized into two primary operating segments: property operations, which includes the long-term ownership, management and leasing of industrial distribution facilities, and the corporate distribution facilities services business (CDFS business), which represents the development of industrial distribution facilities that are either sold to unaffiliated customers or contributed to real estate funds in which ProLogis maintains an ownership interest and acts as manager. The company's been known to hire MBAs with no real estate experience. All openings can be viewed on its web site and applications can be submitted online.

Apartment-focused

AvalonBay Communities, Inc.

Headquarters:
2900 Eisenhower Avenue
Suite 300
Alexandria, VA 22134
Phone: (703) 329-6300
www.avalonbay.com

AvalonBay Communities, Inc. is in the business of developing, redeveloping, acquiring and managing luxury apartment communities in the high barrier-to-entry markets of the United States. These markets are located in the Northeast, Mid-Atlantic, Midwest, Pacific Northwest, and Northern and Southern California regions of the country. At September 30, 2002, AvalonBay owned or held interest in 148 apartment communities containing 43,496 apartment homes in eleven states and the District of Columbia, of which 14 communities were under construction and one was under reconstruction. In addition, the company holds future development rights for 36 communities. All openings can be viewed on the company web site and applications can be submitted online.

Equity Residential

Headquarters:
Two North Riverside Plaza
Suite 450
Chicago, IL 60606
Phone: (312) 474-1300
www.eqr.com

With more than 1,000 properties across 36 states, Equity Residential is the largest publicly traded owner and operator of multifamily properties in the United States. Equity Residential (EQR), formerly known as Equity Residential Properties Trust, is a self-administered and self-managed equity REIT. As of December 31, 2001, the company owned or had interests in a portfolio of 1,076 multi-family properties containing 224,801 apartment units. EQR's properties are located in 36 states with its corporate headquarters in Chicago, Illinois. The company also rents, under operating leases, over 35 divisional, regional and area property management offices throughout the United States. All openings can be viewed on the company site and applications can be submitted online.

Investors and Advisory Firms

Heitman Real Estate Investment Management

Headquarters:
180 North LaSalle Street
Chicago, IL 60601
Phone: (312) 855-5700
www.heitman.com

Heitman is a multinational real estate investment management firm that serves a global client base and makes investments in commercial real estate directly or in publicly traded REIT securities in the U.S. and Europe. All openings can be viewed on the company web site and applications can be submitted online.

Lendlease Real Estate Investments, Inc.

Headquarters:
3424 Peachtree Road N.E.
Atlanta, GA 30326-1102
Phone: (404) 848-8600
www.lendleaserei.com

Lendlease offers real estate investors market presence, product range, investment research, and real estate capabilities with a commitment to providing superior performance and client service through customized programs.

RREEF

Headquarters:
101 California Street
26th Floor
San Francisco, CA 94111
Phone: (415) 781 3300
www.rreef.com

RREEF is a buyer, seller and manager of what is called "investment grade" real estate properties. As of 2003, the company had $17 billion of property under management. RREEF also provides research and other specialized services to REITs. The company is owned by financial services giant Deutsche Bank.

The Blackstone Group

Headquarters:
345 Park Avenue
New York, NY 10154
Phone: (212) 583-5000
www.blackstone.com

The Blackstone Group is of the most active and successful investors in the global real estate market, having completed over 100 separate transactions comprising more than 600 individual real estate assets valued at approximately $13 billion. Through its real estate funds, the firm has raised approximately $4 billion for real estate investments, primarily in North America and Europe. The size of Blackstone Real Estate Advisors' (BREA) investments varies depending on the opportunity and market conditions, but Blackstone generally seeks real estate investments requiring a minimum of $30 million in equity capital. The company is regarded as one of the top dealmakers in the business. Recruits undergraduates and MBAs from top schools.

Walton Street Capital L.L.C.

Headquarters:
900 North Michigan Avenue
Suite 1900
Chicago, IL 60611
Phone: (312) 915-2800
www.waltonst.com

The principals of Walton Street direct the investment and management of the funds. The principals personally make a significant investment in the funds and are compensated through a back-end weighted compensation structure: Fund investors must receive a return of their committed fund capital and a return before any performance fees are paid to the general partner. Of the $1.1 billion of aggregate equity commitments received by the funds, the principals have personally committed $111 million alongside the investors in the funds. The funds have the objective of producing returns to investors of at least 20 percent.

Real Estate Lenders

MetLife Real Estate Investments

Headquarters:
One Madison Avenue
New York, New York 10010
Phone: (212) 578-2211
www.metlife.com

MetLife Real Estate Investments, the real estate investment arm of Metropolitan Life Insurance Company, maintains a portfolio of over $20 billion invested in real estate products including equities, commercial mortgages, and securitized investments. MetLife Real Estate Investments has offices in key cities throughout the United States, as well as London and Toronto. Commercial real estate services include mortgages, leasing, sales, acquisitions and capital transactions.

Northwestern Mutual Life Insurance Company

Headquarters:
720 East Wisconsin Avenue
Milwaukee, WI 53202
Phone: (414) 271-1444
www.northwesternmutualinvestments.com

Northwetern's investment focus includes acquisition and development of commercial property, commercial mortgages and securitized investments. Northwestern Mutual Life places both debt and equity in the real estate market.

Prudential Real Estate Investors

Headquarters
751 Broad Street
Newark, NJ 07102
Phone: (973) 802-6000
HR contact: Sandra Ford
E-mail: sandra.ford@prudential.com
www3.prudential.com/pim/pim/pim_home.html

Prudential was one of the first firms to widely offer the benefits of real estate investing to pension plans. Prudential Real Estate Investors offers a broad range of investment vehicles that endow private and public market opportunities in the U.S., Europe, Asia and Latin America. The product offerings are designed to address specific client needs, including diversified core real estate equity and private debt strategies, value-added real estate equity strategies, and opportunistic or specialized private or public real estate equity strategies. All openings can be viewed on the company site and applications can be submitted online.

Visit Vault at **www.vault.com** for insider company profiles, expert advice,
career message boards, expert resume reviews, the Vault Job Board and more.

VAULT CAREER LIBRARY   **111**

About the Author

Raul Saavedra Jr.

Raul Saavedra Jr. began his real estate career soon after graduating from the University of Illinois in 1994.

Soon after graduating college, Raul bought an apartment building and began working in commercial real estate as an office tenant representation broker. After developing a strong sales and marketing background in real estate, Raul enrolled in The Kellogg School of Management.

Raul has a background in many facets of real estate: residential, commercial, industrial and technology. He has worked at two of the leading commercial real estate firms and was market director for a real estate technology firm.

At Kellogg, Raul became very involved with the real estate club and the curriculum. Raul was a co-chair of both the real estate club and the annual Real Estate Conference. He graduated in June of 2002 and is now a real estate consultant.

Visit Vault at **www.vault.com** for insider company profiles, expert advice, career message boards, expert resume reviews, the Vault Job Board and more.

VAULT CAREER LIBRARY   113

Use the Internet's
MOST TARGETED
job search tools.

Vault Job Board

Target your search by industry, function, and experience level, and find the job openings that you want.

VaultMatch Resume Database

Vault takes match-making to the next level: post your resume and customize your search by industry, function, experience and more. We'll match job listings with your interests and criteria and e-mail them directly to your inbox.

V/\ULT
> the most trusted name in career information™